Stage Jewels

Stefano Papi

Stage Jewels

Through the Careers
of Four Famous
20th Century Sopranos

Foreword by
Pier Luigi Pizzi

Electa

Zoroastro   Dorinda   Angelica

Orlando   Principessa   Medoro

What Stefano Papi doesn't know about jewellery is not worth knowing. And he is also a genuine opera-lover.

Driven by this passion he has painstakingly studied the wardrobes of famous Bel Canto divas in search of the most renowned jewellery designers for the 20th century stage, from Corbella to Marangoni. What he has rediscovered demonstrates the measure of their creativity, based on an incredible amount of historical documentation, while leaving scope for the imagination to run wild.

I have had the pleasure of only meeting two of the four famous singers chosen by Stefano Papi to represent different theatrical periods expressed in terms of the fleeting tastes in stage costume: Rosanna Carteri and Antonietta Stella. I have had to be content with marvelling at the other two, Carosio and Tebaldi, as a member of the audience at so many of their, by now historic, performances.

I met Rosanna Carteri in 1959 at the Maggio Musicale Fiorentino. Handel's *Orlando* was being performed at the Teatro La Pergola, with Rosanna Cartieri as Angelica. She was so young and so beautiful that it was not difficult to fashion the character around her, with all her fascination and seductive power. It was the Brothers Cerratelli who designed her sumptuous baroque costume, using precious Lisio fabrics. The only jewellery used was a necklace with two long rows of large baroque pearls holding a gold-framed cameo borrowed from the painting of a lady by Giovan Battista Tiepolo.

My meeting with Antonietta Stella was at La Scala in Milan for the inauguration of the 1962–63 opera season. On the programme was Verdi's *Il Trovatore* conducted by Gianandrea Gavazzeni and directed by Giorgio de Lullo. I designed the romantic costumes for Leonora by combining 1850s fashion with the Gothic style. They were sumptuous yet austere at the same time.

For her opening aria, "Tacea la notte placida," Antonietta Stella was wearing a silvery pale blue velvet dress that seemed to catch the moon-light, with a black jet stone diadem to hold an immense cloud of black tulle in place over her long dark brown hair—an image that I shall never be able to forget.

In my work I have always sought the essentials, and have gradually become convinced across the years that the only thing that matters in the theatre is what catches the attention of the spectator because of its symbolic, expressive or dramatically clarifying value, or, by its sheer beauty, sets the imagination on fire, becoming an unforgettable emotional experience.

Stefano Papi, in this book, summons up so many forgotten performances that have been bequeathed to history, enabling us to re-live them, seen through his perceptive, nostalgic, marvelling and humourous eyes.

Pier Luigi Pizzi

It was on 21 February 1968 that, barely out of my childhood, I attended my first opera. My parents had taken me to the Teatro dell'Opera in Rome where that evening Antonietta Stella was performing in Umberto Giordano's *Fedora* with Mario Del Monaco.

I was utterly enthralled by that new experience: the atmosphere of the theatre, the sound of the musicians tuning up before the performance, the dimming of the lights, the silence that enveloped the audience as the curtain was about to rise…

Enter Fedora, superb in her sumptuous costumes bedecked by the large parure she has to wear in the first act. I shall never forget my emotional response to hearing her, in the flesh, singing "O grandi occhi lucenti di fede."

Since then, opera has always been one of my great passions, and I still vividly remember that first experience of *Fedora* to this very day. Not only because of the beauty of the music, but also that unique atmosphere which only an Opera House can create. A magical world, that is capable of conjuring up the most powerful emotions. Certainly through the music, but also the scenery, the costumes, the stage jewellery.

I could never have imagined that, as a jewellery expert, I would one day have taken an interest in "mere" imitations. But stage jewels are not mere imitations: they are designed for the stage and for the opera, and they have the same value for them as real jewels. Worn by an artist, they spring to life, conveying and witnessing to emotions, like talismans holding memories of unforgettable moments, successes, fears, applause…

Until some ten years ago it was the custom for established famous singers to have their own wardrobe, which would accompany them everywhere, growing with them as their career progressed: jewels and costumes were lovingly cared for in their private wardrobes. This is how Desdemona eventually wore the same earrings as Violetta, and Tosca had Adriana's necklace, and all these jewellery items followed the singers with them as they toured the world. I have tried to recount a moment in the history of stage jewellery through the careers of four celebrated 20th century sopranos who have opened up their "jewel caskets" for me, displaying their treasures and sharing their memories. I hope that with this I have managed to bring back to life so many unforgettable moments in the history of opera and conveyed these emotions to all opera lovers, to whom I dedicate this book.

Contents

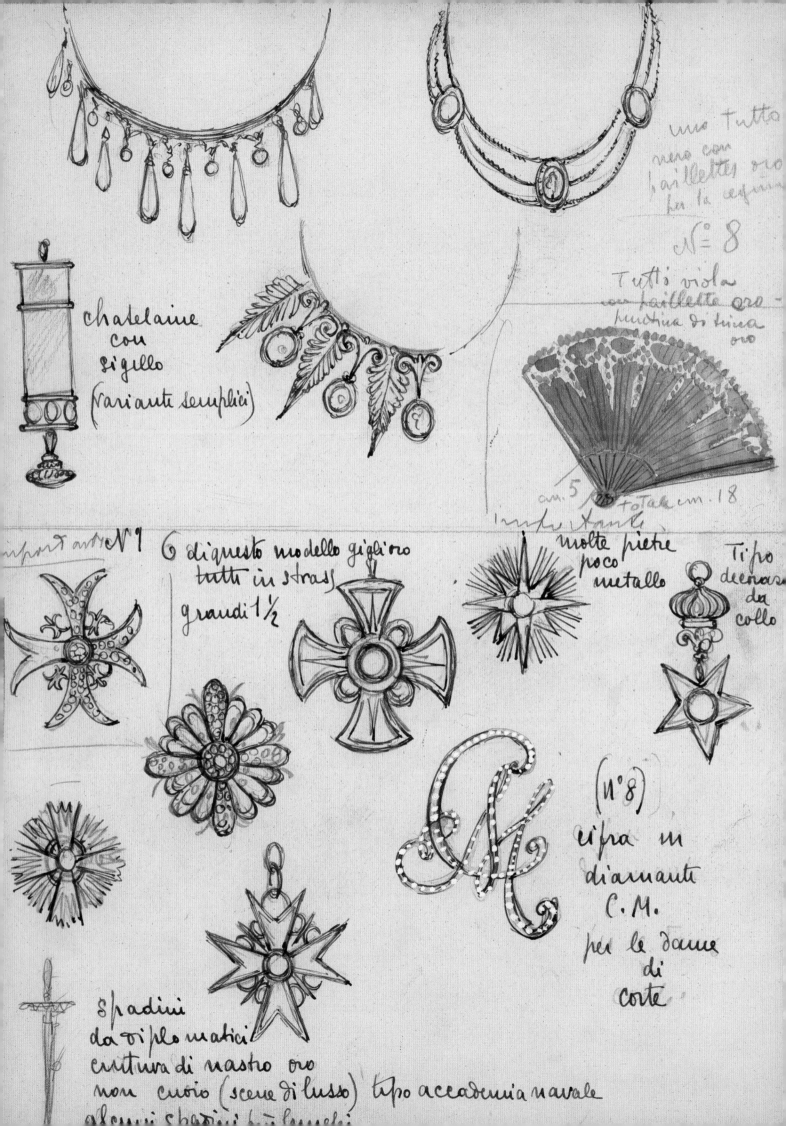

uno tutto nero con paillettes oro per la *[...]*

N° 8

Tutto viola con paillette oro – puntina di tinta oro

chatelaine con sigillo (varianti semplici)

cm 5 *[...]* totale cm. 18

importante

importante N° 1   6 di questo modello giglio oro tutti in strass grandi 1½

molte pietre poco metallo

Tipo decorazione da collo

A (N° 8) cifra in diamante C.M. per le dame di corte

Spadini da diplomatici cintura di nastro oro non cuoio (scene di lusso) tipo accademia navale

Corbella and Caramba
The Fairytale of Stage Jewels
and Costumes in the Golden Age
of Melodrama

In 1865, in Corso Monforte, Milan, Napoleone Corbella founded the first Italian laboratory of stage jewels and weaponry.

This work was continued by his grandson Achille when the firm moved to Via San Paolo. It is thanks to Achille Corbella that the company made a major breakthrough at the beginning of the 20th century, a thriving period for Italian melodrama.

The Milanese laboratory became the most renowned costume house. Not only will La Scala resort to it and become its most prestigious client but the company will also supply other famous "national and foreign theatres."

The creation of a piece of jewellery for the stage is a fascinating activity and the production techniques and methods have remained unchanged since the firm was established.

The stage or costume designer provided the sketch of the piece of jewellery to be created, and this was then produced with pre-formed elements. The technique consisted in placing a brass or Dutch metal sheet inside a press.

The die was then pressed in order to produce an embossed sheet. Once the sheet was removed from the die, it was hand-finished with a bow saw to remove any surplus metal.

This was a lengthy delicate process very similar to the creation of a real piece of jewellery—something unimaginable today for the creation of costume jewellery.

The Corbella firm still keeps samples of the early sheets in its catalogue of the numerous pressed elements used to create many different combinations. The catalogue is arranged by item. It contains elements useful for the creation of Egyptian style jewels or ancient Roman ones, and entire pages show filigree components and Byzantine style brooches.

Prima Fabbrica Italiana di Gioielli ed Armi per Teatro

EREDI DI ACHILLE CORBELLA

CASA FONDATA NEL 1865

STUDIO: Via S. Paolo N. 6 ▲ MILANO ▲ FABBRICA: Bastioni Genova, 31

TELEFONO N. 50-67

FORNITORI DEL TEATRO SCALA E DEI PRINCIPALI TEATRI

ESTERI E NAZIONALI

Angelo Corbella in the early 1930s together with two assistants.

The logo of the firm at the beginning of the century.

Early 20th century sketches, belonging to the Corbella firm, for 18th century-style jewels and decorations.

After defining all the elements, the manufacturing phase proper began.

This atelier however was involved in much more than just the mounting. Traditionally its work was not based just on the costume design. Careful research of specialised texts—such as works on the history of costume—was also needed, for instance, when 18th and 19th century-style jewellery had to be produced. Appropriate sources on the different historical periods were consulted when the pieces of jewellery had to fit a specific setting. Another catalogue displays the finished pieces, presenting page after page of jewellery, arranged by subject.

A catalogue of tiaras contains beautiful pieces of the most diverse styles—such as a First Empire style tiara with cameos set next to crystals, faithfully reproducing the fashion then in vogue. There are tiaras forming arches and spirals, enriched with multi-coloured crystals. To complete the picture, the earring catalogue displays many different styles and shapes to match necklaces and tiaras, making splendid parures.

Sometimes the singers themselves went to the atelier, usually when the costume designer did not specify any particular jewellery but allowed them to choose it themselves, to be worn as the scene required. It should be remembered that in Corbella's contracts with La Scala in Milan it was specified that the jewels provided had to be faithful to the historical period in which the opera was set.

Once the design was produced, all the elements were soldered together. If the jewellery included stones, the settings were soldered to the different parts using tin or silver—although the latter was more difficult and increased the complexity of the work it guaranteed better results.

Once finished, the piece was dipped in a 1 or 2 micron gold or silver electroplating bath. A film of Zappon glue—the same used to fix the stones—was then sprayed on the objects, creating a patina that prevented oxidation and made the gold finish more homogeneous. In the final phase, the artist-craftsmen glued or inserted the stones in the settings closing the claws by hand.

The jewels were then signed by placing a small plate on the back of the piece, with the engraved inscription "A. Corbella, Milano." This hallmark, however, causes some confusion when dating a piece, since alternate generations of the Corbella family had names beginning with the letter "A." An example of the "A. Corbella" hallmark may be found on the back of the diadem on page 128.

On these pages, two early 20th century photographs portraying Saramé Rainold in Richard Wagner's *Lohengrin*, and Bianca Lenzi in Pietro Mascagni's *Isabeau*. They are wearing costumes created by the great stage designer and costumer Caramba and rich stage jewellery, including some large elaborate belts, created by Corbella. In the background, drawings of the same period depicting headdresses.

On the following pages, early 20th century dies for elements of tiaras and brooches displayed next to multi-coloured Bohemian crystals, used at the time by Corbella. The die on the top of page 15 was used in 1912 to create a crown, worn by soprano Maria Farneti for Mascagni's *Isabeau* at La Scala in Milan. The stage costumes had been designed expressly for her by Caramba.

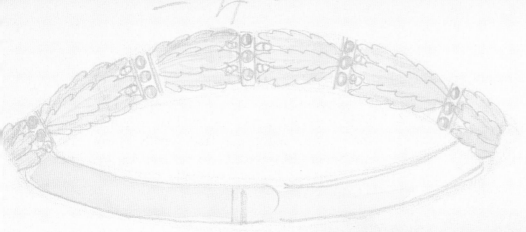

cerchietto di metallo
con foglietle di alloro
e fra esse smeraldi
incastonati a rilievo

A late 19th century photograph showing two parures of jewels created by the Corbella firm, including belts with a long central pendant. In the background, a sketch for a belt pendant.

Early 20th century belt created by the Corbella firm made of colourless Bohemian crystals and silver-plated metal.

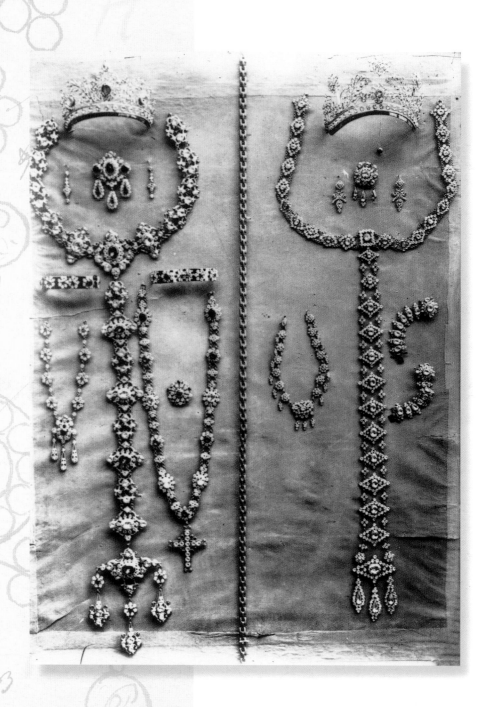

Corbella and Caramba

Adelina Agostinelli Quiroli
in the role of Eva in Richard
Wagner's *Die Meistersinger
von Nürnberg*, wearing a costume
created by Caramba adorned with
a large belt crafted by Corbella.

Early 20th century drawings
for Byzantine-style crowns designed
by the Corbella firm.

On pages 20–21, an original early
20th century drawing belonging
to the Corbella firm and a
photograph of the same period,
belonging to La Scala, portraying
Teresa Cerutti in the *Dance
of Salome*, wearing a headdress
which resembles those shown
on the opposite page.

On pages 22–23, a set of jewels
created by the Corbella firm
at the end of the 1920s for soprano
Rosetta Pampanini performing
the role of Elsa di Brabante
in Richard Wagner's *Lohengrin*
staged in 1929 at La Scala
in Milan. The parure includes
a crown, four bracelets and two large
cloak clasps, created in gilt and
adorned with imitation turquoise
pâte de verre, colourless Bohemian
crystals and imitation pearls.

Corbella and Caramba

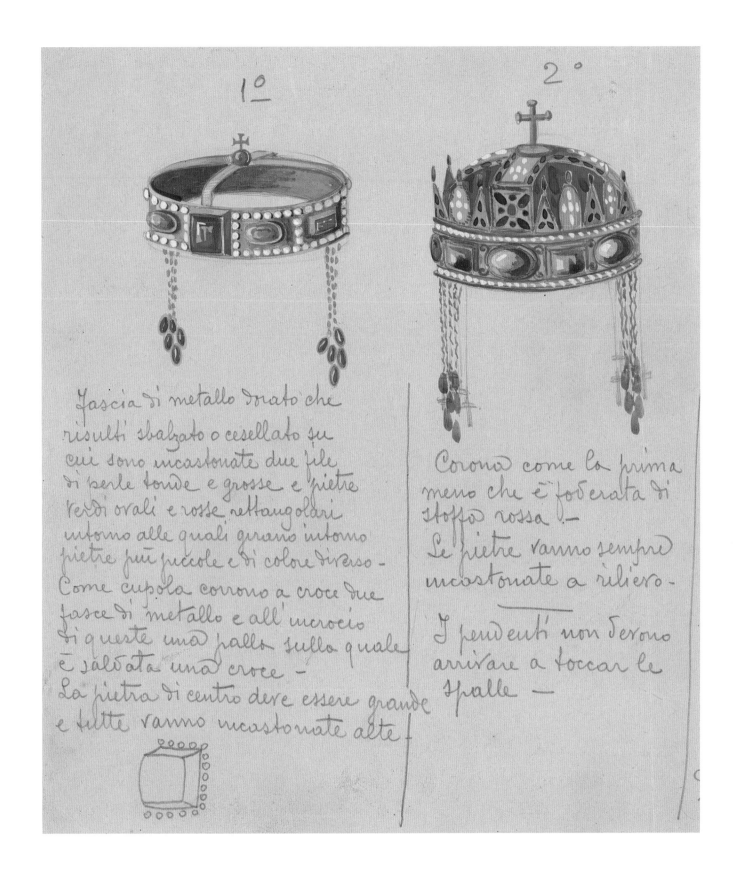

1°

Fascia di metallo dorato che
risulti sbalzato o cesellato su
cui sono incastonate due file
di perle tonde e grosse e pietre
verdi ovali e rosse rettangolari
intorno alle quali girano intorno
pietre più piccole e di colore diverso -
Come cupola corrono a croce due
fasce di metallo e all'incrocio
di queste una palla sulla quale
è salvata una croce -
La pietra di centro deve essere grande
e tutte vanno incastonate alte -

2°

Corona come la prima
meno che è foderata di
stoffa rossa -
Le pietre vanno sempre
incastonate a rilievo -

I pendenti non devono
arrivare a toccar le
spalle -

Corona da donna a forma di diadema
con cerchio che cinge la testa –
Sempre di metallo che paia sbalzato o cesellato
con perle sporgenti e pietre grosse contornate
da piccine –
I pendenti sono snodati ed hanno in punta delle
borchie gemmate – e sono lunghe oltre le spalle –

Corbella and Caramba

Original early 20th century drawings
made by the Corbella firm
depicting jewels and adornments
to be crafted for the role of Dalila
from Saint-Saëns' *Samson et Dalila*.

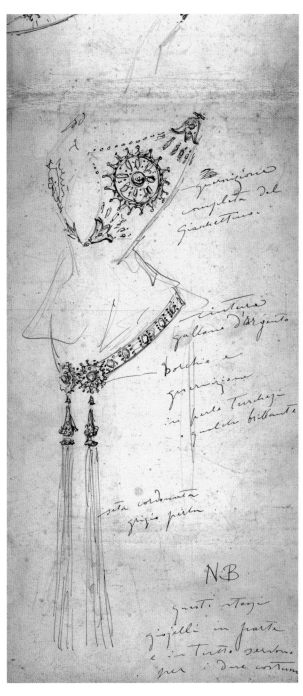

An early 20th century photograph
of soprano Giorgina Caprile playing
the leading role in Massenet's *Thaïs*.
She is wearing stage jewels that show
the richness of the jewellery of that
period.

Corbella and Caramba

A 1907 photograph portraying
a beautiful Lina Cavalieri in the role
of Thaïs, she played at the Paris
Opéra that same year and, the year
before, at the Teatro Carlo Felice,
in Genoa. The soprano was
considered one of the most beautiful
women in the world. She is wearing
a rich headdress part of the stage
jewels created for her role.

A drawing of that same period,
made by the Corbella firm, depicting
jewels with mounted stones.

On the following pages, a headdress
for Giuseppe Verdi's *Aida* created by
Corbella in gilt metal and enamel,
with *pâte de verre* and Bohemian
crystal scarabs, next to the sketches,
dated 1911, of the same adornment
and of other jewels made for the
characters of Aida and Amneris.

On pages 30–31, early 20th century
scarabs and Egyptian-style elements
in Venetian *pâte de verre* shown next
to dies of the same period, which
were used by the Corbella firm to
create jewels in styles like the ones
shown on the previous pages.

In those days the Corbella atelier used Bohemian crystals, but if the jewels required cameos or were Egyptian style with *pâte de verre* scarab plaquettes, they were most often created in Venice. The following pages show some Egyptian-style pieces with scarab-shaped elements or pressed glass plaquettes reproducing the typical designs of that style.

Depending on the scene requirements, metal elements would be enamelled—an example of which is the splendid headdress created in 1911, for Verdi's *Aida* (see following page).

The golden age for Corbella coincided with the rise of the legendary costumer Luigi Sapelli, alias Caramba.

Caramba had proven, from the very start, to be very gifted. His creativity enabled him to sketch caricatures and, soon, to design both scene settings and costumes. He approached the world of journalism when he started to draw caricatures for the *Gazzetta del Popolo* and, subsequently continued with other newspapers until 1896, when he became the editor of the apolitical paper *La Luna*. This assignment paved the way to his appointment as editor of *Pasquino*, for which he not only wrote articles but also continued to draw caricatures.

The doors of the theatre opened wide in 1895, when Sapelli was asked to design and create the scenes and costumes for a new opera: Maestro Berutti's *Taras Bulba*, which was due to go on stage at Teatro Regio in Turin.

Sapelli was given more and more theatre assignments and also, eventually, the great stage settings for D'Annunzio's works.

He established his first atelier for the stage in 1906, in Milan and in 1909 he founded an artistic costume house which was to bear his name. In 1910

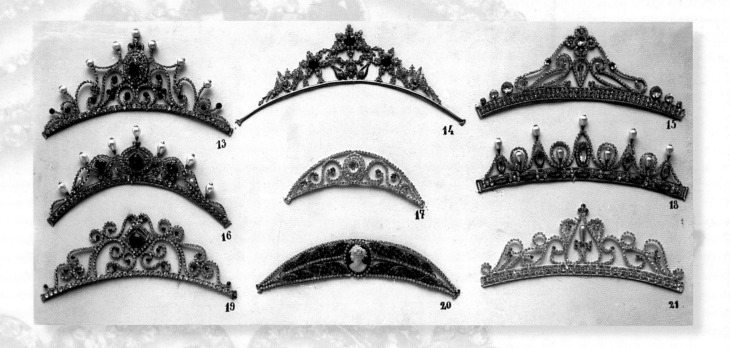

the company hired over 150 employees and started producing about 4,000 costumes a year.

In 1921 he became the art director for stage design at La Scala in Milan. The close co-operation between Corbella and Caramba proved to be very fruitful. Among the best examples of this alliance were the jewels created for Giacomo Puccini's *Turandot*—the great composer's unfinished work, whose grand premiere went on stage at La Scala on 25 April 1926, under the direction of Arturo Toscanini. The prima donna in *Turandot*, Rosa Raisa, wore a big silver-plated headdress adorned with flowers and butterflies mounted *en tremblant*. The headdress matched a large silver-plated collier, studded with crystal stones and pearls, covering her shoulders. The imposing headdress was also decorated with white ostrich feathers.

For the *Turandot* performance another headdress was created, composed of two large pins holding a cascade of pearls and crystals. These jewels were also worn by Bianca Scacciati, the second artist playing *Turandot*, and by Gina Cigna—one of the most

famous Turandots in the history of Italian opera singing—who was to sing this role 493 times throughout her career. In 1948 Maria Callas wore the same jewels at Venice's La Fenice.

Caramba and Corbella worked together on many occasions. Worthy of mention are the beautiful jewels created for Mascagni's *Nerone* in 1935, whose first performance went on stage at Milan's La Scala, under the direction of Mascagni himself. On that occasion, Margherita Carosio, cast in the role of the slave woman Egloge, wore precious jewels (see pages 59 onwards).

Caramba died on 10 November 1936. In his 35-year collaboration with La Scala, he worked on more than 200 stage settings, creating almost all the costumes, jewellery and stage props. Caramba's ingenuity and artistry helped to create some of the most beautiful scene settings at the grand Milanese theatre.

In 1937, Nicola Benois took over, becoming La Scala's new art director. Born in St. Petersburg in 1901, Benois was the son of the great stage designer

Examples of 19th century-style tiaras created by Corbella between the beginning of the 1900s and the 1930s. Pictures from a catalogue such as these were used to show the wide choice to potential costumers, theatres or artists.

At that time, famous singers usually had their own stage wardrobe; costumes were created expressly for the artists and jewels were chosen personally by them.

Corbella and Caramba

A tiara with gilt metal stars and colourless Bohemian crystals, next to one of the sketches for the jewels. Created at the beginning of the 20th century by Corbella. Renata Tebaldi wore this tiara when she played Elisabeth in Richard Wagner's *Tannhäuser* at the Teatro San Carlo, in Naples, in 1948 and asked for two navette-cut Swarovski crystals to be inserted either side of the central star.

Two more examples of tiaras crafted by Corbella at the beginning of the 1900s.

Soprano Rosetta Pampanini made her debut at La Scala singing the role of Cio-Cio-San in Giacomo Puccini's *Madama Butterfly*, conducted by Maestro Arturo Toscanini. She made the first complete recording of this opera (Columbia, 1928, Orchestra and chorus of La Scala, Lorenzo Molajoli conductor). She had an ample voice with a beautiful timbre, a wealth of harmonics and extraordinary acute tones. The legendary soprano Toti dal Monte, at the conference on Toscanini held in Florence in 1967—to which the singers that had sung most frequently with Maestro Toscanini had been invited—said about Pampanini: "The most beautiful acute tones in the world."

She was, in fact, the ideal performer for *Madama Butterfly*, which was successful at La Scala again twenty four years after the failure at that same theatre, in 1904. The story goes that Maestro Puccini, on hearing the catcalls greeting the first performance, said: "Go ahead, shout! In the end we'll see who's right! This is the best opera I have written." After that failure, Puccini revised his opera which originally was in two acts, the second of which was too long; he divided it into two and wrote a prelude to act 3. Shortly after, the opera was successfully performed at the Teatro Grande, in Brescia.

The front page of *Madama Butterfly*'s score with a dedication by Maestro Puccini to Queen Elena of Italy.

Corbella e Caramba

MADAME BUTTERFLY

Stage jewels created by Corbella
at the beginning of the 1930s.
The large necklace was used, in 1933,
by Margherita Carosio in Rossini's
L'Italiana in Algeri on stage
at La Scala. The soprano, shown
on this page on that occasion,
wearing a costume designed specially
for her by Caramba. The headdress
in gilt metal, multi-coloured
Bohemian crystals and imitation
pearls, together with the two large
gilt metal and red *pâte de verre*
bracelets would be worn during
the 1937–38 season by Carosio
in the role of Leila in Bizet's
Les Pêcheurs de Perles on stage
at La Scala. She wore them again,
in the 1950s, at the Teatro San Carlo
in Naples for the same part.

TEATRO ALLA SCALA
MARGHERITA CAROSIO
(Elvira) in *"L'Italiana in Algeri,,*

Fot. M. Camuzzi
della S. A. Crimella

Alexandre, from whom he inherited excellent artistic qualities.

He started collaborating with La Scala in 1926 and in 1927 designing stage settings and costumes for *Boris Godunov* and *Khovanshchina*. His first success at the Milanese theatre came in the 1937–38 season with Rimsky-Korsakov's *Sadko*. Benois would order Corbella elegant Russian-style jewels, like the huge collier illustrated on pp. 80–81.

Nicola Benois held that post for almost 40 years, designing scenes for over 120 memorable performances. Among his many successful creations the splendid design for the stage setting of Donizetti's *Anna Bolena*, in 1957 is worthy of mention: it was directed by Luchino Visconti with Maria Callas in the leading role.

Angelo Corbella, Achille's son, followed in his father's footsteps but moved the atelier to Via Molino delle Armi. Later, the company was inherited by the founder's grandson Achille. After World War II, the production of stage jewellery slowed down coming to a complete halt in the 1950s, when Dina Corbella decided to split up the collection by selling it to several ateliers involved in theatre productions. The firm continued producing only bijouterie.

When Corbella gradually left the scene, another large firm producing stage jewellery started working for La Scala. Established in 1940 by Ennio Marino Marangoni, it had its greatest achievements thanks to its collaboration with Nicola Benois.

Marangoni produced stage jewellery using Swarovski crystals, which resemble natural gems due to their brilliance. Some superb examples of the great craftsmanship of this grand stage jewellery designer may be appreciated in this book on pages 190, 199, 202 and 203.

The long period of collaboration between Benois and Marangoni produced numerous pieces of

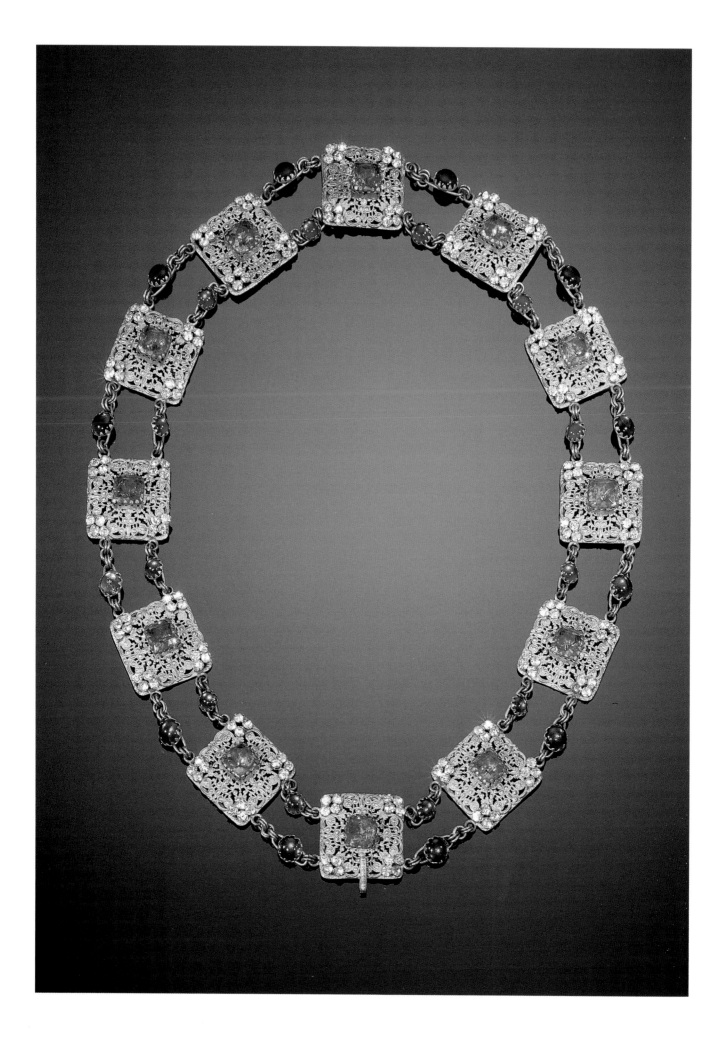

Large belt-necklace with gilt filigree
plates, decorated with imitation
sapphire blue cushion-cut Bohemian
crystals, and blue cabochon-cut *pâte
de verre* and colourless crystals. It
was crafted by Corbella in the 1930s.

Top, a page from Corbella's sample
collection catalogue with diverse
filigree models, among which
are the plates making up the belt.
Bottom, Bohemian crystals used
to decorate the filigree plates.
Early 1900s.

The logo of the stage costume atelier founded by the brilliant stage designer and costumer Caramba in 1909, in Milan.

Margherita Carosio in the role of Gnese she played in 1936 for the grand premiere of Ermanno Wolf-Ferrari's *Il Campiello* at La Scala. The stage jewels were created by Corbella and the magnificent costumes by Caramba. When the costumer saw Margherita in that costume, he exclaimed: "You're my doll!"

Opposite page, Margherita Carosio in the role of Zerlina from Auber's *Fra Diavolo*, in 1934. The soprano is wearing a costume designed specially for her by Caramba; the stage jewels she is modelling are those she also wore in Ermanno Wolf-Ferrari's *Il Campiello*. The parure included the earrings with gilt metal filigree plates and imitation coral beads.

Corbella and Caramba

TEATRO DELLA SCALA - A. XIX
GIANNA PEDERZINI
(*Principessa Fedora Romazov*) in "*Fedora*

FOT. M. CAMUZZI DELLO STAB. FOT. CRIMELLA - MILANO

Mezzo-soprano Gianna Pederzini in the role of Princess Fedora Ramazov in Umberto Giordano's *Fedora* on stage in Milan, at La Scala, in 1939. She is wearing a large headdress which resembles a Russian *kokoshnik*, created by the Corbella firm in gilt metal, colourless and green Bohemian crystals and imitation pearls. The artist is also wearing a brooch with a large cross pendant with six arms decorated in the same style (opposite page), crafted by Corbella. Pederzini offered these jewels as a good-luck token to Antonietta Stella who wore them at the Teatro Regio, in Turin, for her debut in the role of Fedora.

Corbella and Caramba

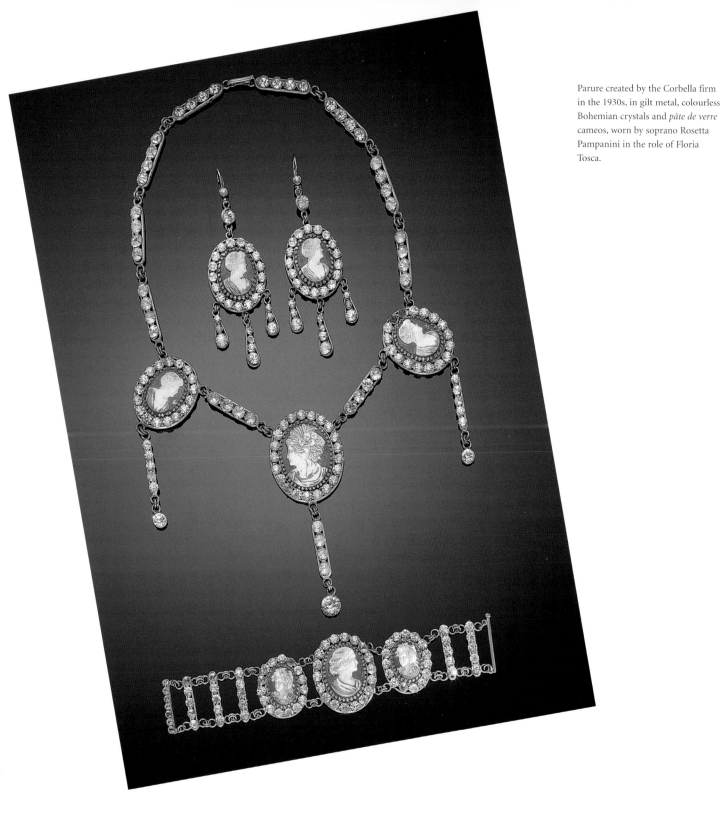

Parure created by the Corbella firm in the 1930s, in gilt metal, colourless Bohemian crystals and *pâte de verre* cameos, worn by soprano Rosetta Pampanini in the role of Floria Tosca.

wonderful stage jewellery. Among them, it is worth mentioning those created during the 1952–53 season for a *Boris Godunov* performance. In a letter sent to Marangoni, Benois himself expressed his great admiration for such an exquisite creation.

Equally memorable are the jewels Maria Callas wore in 1956 for a *Fedora* performance for which, together with a very big diadem, Marangoni created a necklace holding an Orthodox cross, that looked very much like the one Renata Tebaldi would wear in 1961, when she played the same role

at the Teatro San Carlo in Naples. And again, the jewels designed for Anna Bolena in 1957 as well as the extraordinary headdress worn by Birgit Nilsson in *Turandot*, whose design was produced by Benois and the artist Chou-Ling.

Corbella and Marangoni, however, were not the only ones to produce stage jewellery. Other great master craftsmen supplied splendid adornments to be worn by the greatest singers at unforgettable performances that were to spark audiences' imagination all over the world.

Soprano Margherita Carosio portrayed at La Scala in the role of Norina in Donizetti's *Don Pasquale*, and the costume, created by Caramba, she wore for that role. The soprano is also wearing the necklace on page 71 and a tiara created by the Corbella firm for that costume.

On page 48, the *pâte de verre* cameos were dyed in different colours according to the colour of the costume and the designer's specifications.

On page 49, a magnificent parure created by the firm Corbella in the early 1900s, in gilt metal, colourless crystals and cameos. It comprises necklace, earrings, two bracelets and a large tiara with laurel leaves and a central cameo, not shown here. All the jewels bear the hallmark "A. Corbella, Milano."

Corbella e Caramba

FOT. M. CAMUZZI
DELLA S. A. CRIMELLA

TEATRO ALLA SCALA - 1935-36
MARGHERITA CAROSIO
(Norina) in "Don Pasquale"
COSTUMI DI CARAMBA

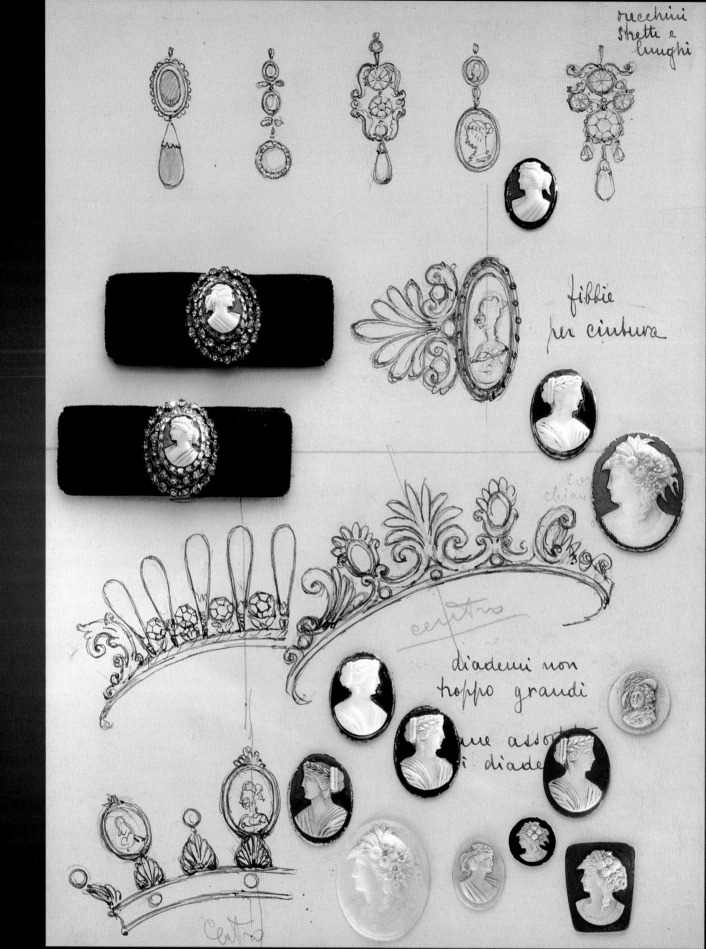

orecchini
stretti e
lunghi

fibbie
per cintura

con
chiar

centro

diademi non
troppo grandi

ne assort
i diade

Centro

Opposite page, a portrait of mezzo-soprano Giulietta Simionato in *Fedora*, in the 1940s. The artist is wearing a pair of earrings created by Corbella in colourless and aquamarine Bohemian crystals set in gilt metal.

Bottom, Margherita Carosio in 1937 in the film *Regina della Scala*, wearing the earrings created by Corbella with strings of colourless crystals set in gilt metal.

Two pages of the vast sample catalogue of earrings created by the Corbella firm.

A beautiful portrait of Maria Callas when she made her debut in the role of Leonora in Giuseppe Verdi's *Il Trovatore*, performed on 20 June 1950 at Palacio de las Bellas Artes, in Mexico City. The cast included mezzo-soprano Giulietta Simionato, tenor Kurt Baum and baritone Leonard Warren, conducted by Maestro Picco. Callas is wearing an elegant 1940s style necklace, in silver-plated metal and imitation diamond colourless crystals, and a costume which was part of her personal stage wardrobe, which she wore also in other performances of *Il Trovatore*. She wore it at the opening of La Scala on 7 December 1951 when she played Elena in Giuseppe Verdi's *I Vespri Siciliani*, conducted by Maestro Victor de Sabata. Maria Callas, who was to become a legend in the opera world, wore that necklace again on her debut at the Teatro Comunale in Florence in a role which would become her favourite—Violetta in Giuseppe Verdi's *La Traviata*. Her performance on 28 May 1955 at La Scala, in Milan—Luchino Visconti director and Carlo Maria Giulini conductor—will go down in history, along with the magnificent costumes designed by Lila De Nobili.

La Traviata and *Norma* were the operas the soprano sang most frequently. From the end of the 1940s to the beginning of the 1950s, Renata Tebaldi, her only rival in the world of opera, would wear in several performances—from *La Traviata* to *Falstaff* and *Adriana Lecouvreur*—a necklace exactly like this one (see page 188). At the time, it was usual for artists to wear their own stage jewels, thus making a greater impact on spectators, regardless of the historic period of the opera.

Corbella and Caramba

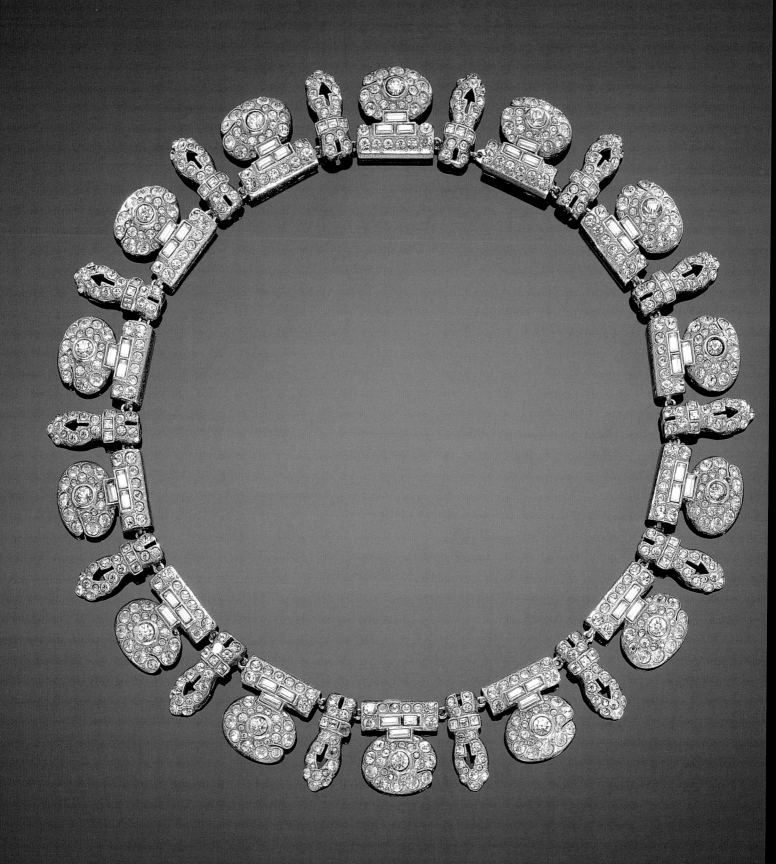

Margherita Carosio

"Even as a child I was fascinated whenever I watched my father giving lessons to young singers. I have always been fond of music and loved singing. But, what really made me be so keen on singing was an old record I listened to, played over and over again by our next-door neighbours. The aria which intrigued me, was "Vieni al tempio," from Vincenzo Bellini's *I Puritani*, sung by the famous Amelita Galli-Curci. At some point, I decided to borrow that record for a few days, listen to it carefully and then sing the romance just like the soprano sang it. When I gave the record back to my neighbour, and sang the romance to thank him, he was stunned by my performance, something still very far from the celebrated Galli-Curci's!" Margherita Carosio remembers.

She was born in Genoa on 7 June 1908, and her father Natale was a musician and singing teacher. He realised very early how gifted she was and gave Margherita her first singing lessons. As a young girl she was enrolled at the Nicolò Paganini Conservatory where she started studying violin with Maestro Parodi. At 16 she was awarded her first diploma in "Singing, piano, harmony and composition" and made her debut in the operatic world at the Teatro Cavour in Novi Ligure.

The singer recalls the great excitement she felt on that occasion. Only a few months earlier she had sung at a concert at the Paganini Conservatory and an impresario who had listened to her was so impressed by her singing talent that he promised to give her the main role in an opera. In fact he kept his promise and offered her a part in the third performance of Donizetti's *Lucia di Lammermoor*.

That was not an easy day for Margherita. The score of the opera was nowhere to be found and her father had to replace the prompter at the last minute. The impresario, afraid that the young girl would not make it to the end of the performance, asked the soprano who had sung in the two previous performances to stand by, in case she had to replace Margherita. The atmosphere was tense, but she was the only calm one, producing her first triumphant performance.

The artist admits that playing Lucia has been very emotional for her ever since that day. "When the curtains fell for the first time," she recalls, "I felt the tension that had sustained me until then, dissolve. The applause I heard made me feel I had to keep my promise. Then, my joy became almost explosive and I felt ecstatic. I could have hugged all the spectators as a sign of my gratitude for the appreciation they were so generously expressing and for making me feel so reassured. I have always sung for my audiences ever since —for each and every person in the hall—reaching the hearts of those who were listening to me."

Hard times, however, followed that first successful performance, long hours spent in waiting rooms, anxiety before auditions, the discouragement after the unfairness of the early days…

There is one episode the artist will never forget: "One day I was called in for an audition. I was supposed to replace a famous artist who had fallen ill. Next to me there was another young woman whom I knew had very strong backers. I had just had a recent successful performance in that same province and for that reason I felt more confident and bold. I started singing knowing that I was there to make a good showing. When the test was over, I felt I had won. I was so happy. However, the other candidate was selected! At first I was more astonished than sorry. But soon I started to feel resentful. Yet the sense of being victorious remained and has made me stronger ever since. These resources might appear inconsistent, but they are instinctive and absolutely necessary for a profession where one moment of despair may translate into years of inactivity."

Subsequently, Margherita sang in *Il Barbiere di Siviglia* and in *Lucia di Lammermoor* in Friuli, and in *Rigoletto* in Pavia. But the artist's real stepping-stone on the path to success was her performance in Puccini's *La Bohème*, in 1928. The young artist was called by the impresario Ferone to interpret the role of Musetta at the Teatro Grande, in Brescia. In the stalls was the famous soprano Margaret Sheridan, who had been appointed by Covent Garden in London to look for new singing talent. Sheridan was so impressed by Margherita's voice and by the spontaneity in her interpretation that she helped the young artist to sign a contract and play the role of Musetta at the famous Covent Garden in the 1928 season. The cast of that *Bohème* was prestigious: directed by Maestro Vincenzo Bellezza, Sheridan sang the role of Mimì and Aureliano Pertile—"Toscanini's tenor"—played Rodolfo. That performance was very emotional for Margherita, who still recalls when, after the premiere, the artists were introduced to King George V and Queen Mary.

Again at Covent Garden, immediately after *Bohème*, Margherita sang the role of Zarevich in Mussorgsky's *Boris Godunov*, alongside the legendary Feodor Chaliapin, in a three-language version. Chaliapin sang in Russian, Carosio in Italian and the chorus in French. Margherita Carosio admits that meeting that great opera singer represented a turning point for her artistic training. As she states, it was Chaliapin who made her fully understand what *becoming* a character meant, rather than just *interpreting* it.

In the first year spent in Milan, Margherita applied for auditions to theatre agencies as well as to La Scala, to be evaluated by Maestro Toscanini. At that time, Margherita lived with her mother in a boarding house on Via Torino, which catered for artists. Days went by. Eventually, one day, when she was eating a dish of *peperonata* (a red and yellow pepper ratatouille with strong seasoning)—a funny detail the artist will not forget!—, their doorbell rang. It was a messenger boy from La Scala who informed Margherita she had been invited, that same afternoon at 4 o'clock, to an audition with Maestro Toscanini (and the *peperonata* was certainly not the best dish to have before an audition!).

When Margherita Carosio arrived at La Scala she made arrangements with the pianist that was to accompany her. She recalls that a tenor and a baritone were scheduled to sing before her that same afternoon, but never showed up. The audition took place before Maestro Toscanini and the former baritone Scandiani (at the time director of La Scala), who sat at the back of the hall.

Margherita started singing the aria "Come per me sereno" from *La Sonnambula*. The Maestro asked her to continue with the cabaletta. At the end of the audition, Toscanini interrupted the assistant who had been following him with the notebook containing the ritual questions to interview the singers. He approached the artist—who still gets very emotional when she remembers the Maestro staring at her—and said: "This girl's name will shine in golden letters in the sky of opera singing." The dream of en-

STAGIONE LIRICA
ARENA DI VERONA
MARGHERITA CAROSIO
IN
RIGOLETTO

FOTO BERTOLAZZI - VERONA

Carosio in 1933, performing in
Giuseppe Verdi's *Rigoletto* at the
Arena di Verona. The soprano played
the role of Gilda and Beniamino
Gigli that of the Duke.

Margherita Carosio in one of her
first performances as Rosina
in Gioacchino Rossini's *Il Barbiere
di Siviglia*.

tering the gate of Via Filodrammatici had come true for Margherita—the doors of the most famous theatre in the world were now open before her.

Margherita Carosio, however, never experienced the joy of being directed by the great Maestro. She recalls that Toscanini left Italy in 1929 to go to the United States, where he became the New York Philharmonic Symphony Orchestra's resident director. He was, however, kept informed about what was going on at La Scala by Riboldi, a lawyer who married the singer Maria Farneti.

The Maestro used to travel to Salzburg every year to conduct *Falstaff*, in which the great Mariano Stabile sang the main role. One day Riboldi called Carosio into his offices to give her a letter from the Maestro who was inviting her to sing the role of Nannetta in *Falstaff*, in Salzburg. Carosio, albeit flattered, turned down the offer—not knowing what the effects might have been—because she did not feel ready for that role.

However, that refusal was not without consequences. In the 1935 season of La Scala, Maestro De Sabata was to conduct *Falstaff* and the role of Nannetta was assigned to an American artist who, at the last minute, did not turn up. A good substitute was nowhere to be found, so Maestro De Sabata and director Frigerio begged Carosio to accept. The singer had just had a successful performance in Mascagni's *Nerone* and accepted their offer. She was a resounding success, especially when she sang the romance "Sul fil d'un soffio esteso," in the last act. Nevertheless, when Maestro Toscanini found out that Carosio had accepted to play Nannetta with Maestro De Sabata, he felt offended. When he came back to Italy in 1946, to conduct in the opening concert after the restoration of La Scala, Carosio wrote him a letter to explain what had happened and returned from Naples, where she had been singing, to attend the event.

Margherita played a role at La Scala as the page Oscar in Giuseppe Verdi's *Un Ballo in Maschera* as a stand in. Carosio recalls that, some time after the audition, she received a phone call from Antonio Barbato, secretary to Aureliano Pertile, who asked her if she knew that role. The soprano didn't want to miss that opportunity and lied, answering she knew it very well: she ended up studying hard to learn it very quickly. She succeeded. The cast was exceptional: Aureliano Pertile, Giannina Arangi-Lombardi and Carlo Galeffi. The latter was one of the most important baritones of the time and the two immediately made friends.

Carosio as Egloge in Pietro Mascagni's *Nerone*, which had its premiere in 1935 at La Scala in Milan. The Maestro said of the young opera singer: "What a singer! And what a performer! She is like a dream, being carried on the voice of the soul." In the background, the third scene of the opera based on sketches made by Edoardo Marchioro. Costumes were created by Caramba and jewels by the Corbella firm.

That performance marked the beginning of Margherita's successful career at La Scala.

In 1933, she was a memorable Filina in Ambroise Thomas' *Mignon* with Tito Schipa in the role of Guglielmo and Gianna Pederzini as the leading character. Caramba designed the costumes. Carosio well recalls that when the costumer saw her wearing his creations, he told her: "You are my doll."

Franco Abbiati wrote in the newspaper *Corriere della Sera*: "Margherita Carosio, a lively sparkling Filina, was applauded during her performance in particular when she sang the difficult polonaise in the second act." In the same season, at La Scala, Margherita played the role of Elvira in Gioacchino Rossini's *L'Italiana in Algeri,* alongside Francesco Manurita, one of the most celebrated tenor interpreters of Lindoro in that opera.

In 1933 she was Inès at the Arena di Verona in Meyerbeer's *L'Africaine*, with Beniamino Gigli, conducted by Sergio Failoni. Margherita recalls when she was in Parma with the great tenor taking part in a concert celebrating Verdi before an enthusiastic audience: "It was one of those vibrant events, when artists and audience become one and sway along with the music. At the end of the concert, the crowd walked with us all the way back to our hotel. Among the fans there were also young men who were very, very fond of music. How could we thank them? Gigli had an idea, 'By singing!' So we walked out on the balcony of the hotel and he began to sing a Neapolitan song. Then it was my turn, and I sang Lucia's rondo. We ended up being greeted by thunderous applause."

In the 1933–34 season Carosio played Zerlina in a superb *Fra Diavolo*, by Auber, together with Aureliano Pertile and with imaginative costumes designed for her by the talented Caramba.

The 1934–35 La Scala season produced a memorable performance, which crowned her as the prima donna of opera. Mascagni's *Nerone* had its premiere on 16 January 1935. The composer himself—who started writing the score in 1892—conducted it. The libretto had been composed by Giovanni Targioni Tozzetti according to the purest late 19th-century style, in perfect harmony with the highly melodramatic style of the composition and Mascagni's own goal: "I want to save all I can of traditional Italian melodrama." Edoardo Marchioro created superb scenes (especially the Domus Aurea terrace); and the costumes and settings made by Corbella were fan-

Margherita Carosio

Margherita Carosio

The original La Scala bill
for the grand premiere of Mascagni's
Nerone.

Mascagni's dedication on the score
of the opera, given as a present by
the composer to Margherita Carosio.

The young artist portrayed with
Maestro Mascagni, tenor Aureliano
Pertile (Nerone), baritone Granforte
and bass Vaghi in the performance
at the Teatro Reale dell'Opera
in Rome, in 1936.

On the opposite page, Carosio
as Egloge in the film *Regina della
Scala* of 1937. She is wearing earrings
crafted by Corbella in gilt metal
and imitation pearls.

tastic, while the direction by Mario Frigerio was simply perfect. Aureliano Pertile played the role of Nerone, while Margherita Carosio was Egloge, the slave woman. The singer recalls that the performance was so successful that many baby girls born during that period were named after Egloge.

That grand premiere generated great expectations and spectators came from all over the world. Margherita had an overwhelming success, confirmed unanimously by the audience, critics and the national and international press. The *Daily Mail* correspondent wrote: "The performance of the premiere was perfect … Margherita Carosio was the star of the evening." Alceo Toni, from *Il Popolo d'Italia* commented: "Margherita Carosio's Egloge was tender and melodious, her singing sheer bliss. The artistic ability in her voice, the clear brilliance of its sound, and its charming expressiveness contributed greatly to the success of the performance." Carlo Frattini continued in the pages of *Il Sole*: "A personal success for Margherita Carosio, as Egloge. In her delicate aria and duet she achieved very melodious tone that was truly moving, well deserving the long applause that followed."

The following year, *Nerone* was on at the Teatro Reale dell'Opera in Rome, under the direction of the composer himself, and with Aureliano Pertile in the starring role. After the successful performance in Rome, Lucio d'Ambra wrote in *Corriere della Sera*: "In the

second act, Egloge, her voice and great charm have enchanted everyone in the city of Rome at once." He then continued by saying that Pietro Mascagni, surrounded by friends and admirers in his dressing-room after his triumph, said about Carosio: "What a singer! And what a performer! It is like a dream, being carried in the voice of a soul!"

It was that very triumphant performance that opened the gates of Hollywood to Margherita Carosio. Metro Goldwin Mayer offered her a fantastic contract, on condition that she left immediately for the United States and stayed there for at least six months. Margherita was thrilled and flattered, but her affection for her country—which she had never left for such a long period of time—and her boyfriend, who would have never accepted such a separation, made her turn down the offer. She gave up the idea of going to Hollywood and a movie career to get married instead. Yet, in 1937, Cinecittà opened the doors to the artist and Carosio would be the "Regina della Scala" in the film of the same name, directed by Camillo Mastrocinque.

In 1936, another grand premiere at La Scala starred Margherita as Gnese, in Ermanno Wolf-Ferrari's *Il Campiello*, directed by Mario Ghisalberti. The singer wore fabulous costumes designed by Caramba and jewellery created by Corbella. Goldoni's comedy, adapted into a libretto by Mario Ghisalberti—a fel-

low Venetian, like the composer and the scene designer Pierretto Bianco—was a great triumph. Critics declared: "The mise-en-scène and the performance of *Il Campiello* at La Scala are the best a spectator can expect." The author wrote on the score he gave Margherita: "To my marvellous Gnese, Margherita Carosio, as a token of the beautiful evening of 12 February 1936. Yours, Ermanno Wolf-Ferrari."

The artist recalls with pleasure an episode that occurred in Venice, where she went to sing at La Fenice. She was sitting in a café and the waiter, who had not recognised her, was telling a client: "Doctor, you should go to La Fenice for *Il Campiello*. It is really worth seeing. And when Carosio sings, in the last act, she is really moving…"

During that same season she played the role of Vivetta in Francesco Cilea's *L'Arlesiana* alongside Tito Schipa and the part of Aminta in Richard Strauss' *Die sweigsame Frau*, a new opera for La Scala again under the direction of Marinuzzi. The author congratulated Carosio and posed for pictures with her. She also sang the part of Norina in Donizetti's *Don*

Carosio in 1933 in the role of Filina
in Ambroise Thomas' *Mignon*
on stage at La Scala where she sang
next to Tito Schipa (Guglielmo).
On the right, a portrait with
dedication: "To Filina Carosio
from Guglielmo Schipa" and another
one depicting the two singers.
The costumes were created by
Caramba and the jewels by Corbella.

On the following pages, the parure
created by Corbella in gilt metal
and colourless Bohemian crystals
decorated with stars which,
on the tiara, where mounted
en tremblant in order to make them
vibrate every time the artist moved.
The mace bears the hallmark
"A. Corbella, Milano."

Margherita Carosio

Pasquale, where she wore the costumes designed exclusively for her by Caramba and the stage jewels created by Corbella. Francesco Abbiati wrote in *Corriere della Sera*: "Margherita Carosio literally threw the audience into ecstasy with the liveliness of her singing, so clearly and lightly modulated."

In 1937, she added to her repertoire the role of Gretel in Engelbert Humperdinck's *Hänsel und Gretel*, which she sang with Gianna Pederzini.

That same year, Margherita sang in Rome at a concert at the Accademia di Santa Cecilia. The concert was "full of technical complexities." In the first part, a classical repertoire was to be performed, followed by music by Saint-Saëns, Donizetti, Gounod and concluded by pieces by the most famous modern composers: Lualdi, Pizzetti, Persico, Respighi, and Paribeni. Rome's daily paper *Il Messaggero*, in an article of 31 December 1937, reported: "Albeit young, the soprano Margherita Carosio has been admired as a true diva of our operatic world, and that is exactly how she appeared yesterday, at Santa Cecilia, where she performed in a programme of old, modern and contemporary music. Her singing is always graceful both when she has to bring out the pure virtuosity of a passage and when she has to evoke and bring to life the emotion in music, whether it is archaic or modern. The virtuoso quality of her talent was fully revealed in "Regnava nel silenzio" in Donizetti's *Lucia* as well as in Gounod's waltz in *Roméo et Juliette*, and in Saint-Saëns' *Le Rossignol et la Rose*. On those occasions, she absolutely fascinated the spectators, performing trills, semi-toned scales and extremely difficult passages with extraordinary ease. She also performed Scarlatti's and Haydn's music with exquisite grace and a divine voice. Her lyrical sentiment has faithfully evoked scores by Lualdi, Pizzetti, Persico, Respighi and Paribeni."

During same year, Margherita Carosio was also triumphant at the Teatro Colón, in Buenos Aires, in the role of the Princess of Shemakha in Rimsky-Korsakov's *The Golden Cockerel*. In the 1937–38 season, at La Scala she sang in Rossini's *Il Barbiere di Siviglia* with Tito Schipa; in Bizet's *Les Pêcheurs de Perles*—scenes of which were based on Brunelleschi's sketches—and, finally, in the role of Fiordispina in Cimarosa's *L'Impresario in Angustie*.

That same season, she was Princess Volkhova in a new opera that was put on at La Scala, namely, Rimsky-Korsakov's *Sadko*, under the direction of Gino Marinuzzi and with Nicola Benois—who had replaced Caramba after his death—as scenographer and stage designer. Benois, of Russian origins, was

Carosio in the film *Regina della Scala* wearing the pendant earrings created by Corbella (on this page), which she had already used when she played the role of Filina. She is also wearing a Bohemian crystal necklace with *pâte de verre* cameos, designed by Caramba for the role of Norina in Donizetti's *Don Pasquale* for the 1935–36 season at La Scala. The red velvet dress was decorated with cameos, like the ones on the necklace. In her hair, a colourless Bohemian crystal chain created by Corbella in the mid-1920s, used by the artist in several operas and concerts.

On pages 70–71 these jewels are shown next to another necklace, also created by Corbella, with imitation ruby crystals mounted on gilt metal settings. In the centre, early 20th century earrings mounted on silver with colourless crystals.

Margherita Carosio

Margherita Carosio in some pictures of 1937 during the shooting of the film *Regina della Scala*, in a 18th century-style costume donned by the artist for the scenes in which she sang *L'Europa Riconosciuta*, the dramatic opus written by abbot Mattia Verazi and set to music by Antonio Salieri, which opened La Scala on 3 August 1768. The theatre had been built on the site of the church of Santa Maria della Scala whose construction was ordered by Regina della Scala, wife of Bernabò Visconti, in 1381.

greatly appreciated for his scenes evoking the typical settings of his homeland and for the magnificent and lively costumes of the characters that perfectly suited the scenes. Corbella continued to design and craft the required jewellery.

In April 1939, Maestro Gino Marinuzzi brought Giovanni Paisiello's *Il Barbiere di Siviglia* out of obscurity especially for Margherita Carosio, who played the role of Rosina.

Throughout Carosio's career some critics maintained that *Lucia di Lammermoor* was one of her fortes. On 15 March 1939, Guido Pannain wrote in Naples' daily paper *Il Mattino*: "The revival of an opera like *Lucia* can be justified only when there is a protagonist capable of personifying the stylistic and musical spirit specific to the drama. Margherita Carosio artistically achieved that yesterday. She is the real incarnation of Bel Canto that she revives according to Italian traditions. Its beauty is not based on the acrobatic emptiness of cold perfection but, rather, on the intrinsic resonance which the soul bestows to the sound. Margherita Carosio is gifted with light-ca-

denced virtuosities, agility and dazzling tones above the register, as well as the expressive and stirring sweetness of *canto legato*. She has a lightness that eschews superficiality of interpretation, in favour of melody and grace. Her Lucia is delicately pallid and suffering. The intimate tragedy of a naive soul pulsates in the brilliant vibrations of her singing. Her delightful timbre is equal to the charm of her character, her graceful voice stands out and defines her stage persona." Two years later, the same music critic wrote in *Il Mattino* after another performance of *Lucia*: "Margherita Carosio is the precious gem of our opera. Her delicate and melodious voice resonates anew, each time you listen to it, with the beautiful feelings of nostalgia and memory … Margherita Carosio is a singer in the purest and highest sense of the word, whose expressive potential and artistry — based on genuine musical talent—are above any virtuosity. Yesterday, after the delirium scene it was the audience she actually made delirious!"

Genoa's daily paper *Il Secolo XIX* wrote on 29 May 1939: "Praising Carosio is superfluous. She is a del-

Margherita Carosio

Opposite page, a stage costume created for the film *Regina della Scala* in purple velvet with crystal embroideries of the same shade, worn by Carosio in a scene of the film.

icate, exquisite singer, a very bright and expansive artist. She infuses her performances with deep vibrant life-like emotions. Last night, personifying Lucia, she lived her role with great expressive intensity, and the audience responded with genuine enthusiasm."

On that same day in Genoa, *Il Nuovo cittadino* reported: "The evening of 28 May 1939 will be a landmark in the history of Genoese theatre, as one of those memorable dates evoking the triumphs of the most remarkable singers that marked the end of the 19th century and the beginning of the 20th. Margherita Carosio appeared as a particularly attractive Lucia—elegant, graceful with her imposing figure—but especially with that profound and exquisite sense of humanity she conveys to her character … Her argentine voice—melodious and sweet —is never forced to the middle notes or to other tonalities but springs spontaneous, pure and faithful to the author's text with clear, soft and warm accents. The high notes—the highest ones for the register of a soprano surprise listeners because of their clarity, the trills, *spiccatos* with the precious and enchanting *fioritura* of her truly matchless virtuosity. Her singing expresses her beautiful emotions and feelings."

In the 1938–39 season at La Scala Carosio played Amina in Vincenzo Bellini's *La Sonnambula*. In January 1939, Ildebrando Pizzetti wrote in Rome's *La Tribuna*: "Margherita Carosio was an adorable Amina. She sang the role as perhaps no other artist would sing it today: with a lively gracefulness, with

Carosio in the part of Leila in Georges Bizet's *Les Pêcheurs de Perles* performed at La Scala in the 1937–38 season. Costumes and scenes were based on designs made by Brunelleschi and the jewels were created by Corbella.

An overview of act 1 of the opera.

The necklace created by Corbella for the artist singing the role of Leila. It is made of gilt metal plates (shown also in the sample catalogue on page 41) decorated with colourless and multi-coloured imitation diamond Bohemian crystals. The central piece bears the mark "A. Corbella, Milano" on the reverse.

MARGHERITA CAROSIO
Leila in "I Pescatori di Perle"
TEATRO DELLA SCALA
STAGIONE LIRICA - ANNO XVI

112
ITALFOTO

TEATRO DELLA SCALA - STAGIONE LIRICA - ANNO XVI
I PESCATORI DI PERLE - DI G. BIZET
SCENE SU BOZZETTI DI U. BRUNELLESCHI
ITALFOTO
ATTO I
115

a moving tenderness, with a pure, beautiful voice that was enchanting. She has adorned the melodies, in their cadences, with golden filigrees and ornaments of pearls and diamonds, which evoke the great bygone singers—Malibran, Pasta, Albani, Patti or Pinkert. But Carosio has also been the admirable interpreter of the character of the opus, and not only in the first act—so idyllic and joyful—but also in the second and third acts which are full of pathos and emotion. She was commendable, with her artistry, when the piece required her to change expression and acting, from recitative to recitative and from aria to aria."

Carlo Gatti, referring to *La Sonnambula,* in *L'Illustrazione italiana* on 8 January 1939 wrote: "Miss Margherita Carosio, the protagonist, is now the favourite of La Scala. A lively voice, warm expression, artistry and graceful figure—these are the qualities which distinguish her and include her in the roll of our most celebrated singers." The *Corriere della Sera* wrote: "Carosio, lively yet restrained, highly emotional yet astonishing, controlled and modulated, was an extremely beautiful Amina to admire and listen to. She has graciously animated the stage, filling it with tremolos and arpeggios, trills and vibratos, almost transforming it in a divine aviary."

In May 1939, Margherita sang in a concert at the Naples Conservatory, directed by Maestro Tullio Serafin. *Il Mattino* reported on the event: "The main part of the programme was based on the first performance of Giovanni Pascoli's short poem *Paulo Uccello,* which Guido Pannain set to music for soprano, chorus and orchestra … Margherita Carosio is the perfect singer. This wonderful artist combines a special musicality with the brilliance of a splendid voice, homogenous in all its registers, whose timbre is a soft caress to your ears. No better balance could be found between the accents suitable to render both the purity of mystical feeling and the warmth of interior poetic human emotion."

Guido Pannain, a great admirer of Margherita and her musical talent, was inspired by the artist when he composed *Beatrice Cenci* in 1942. Carosio interpreted Beatrice in the grand premiere at the Teatro San Carlo in Naples that same year and, the following year, at the Teatro Reale dell'Opera in Rome.

In 1940 in that same theatre she sang Ottorino Respighi's *La Campana Sommersa* interpreting the role of the fairy Rautendelein. The Maestro wrote to her: "What did you think of Carosio? I found her simply adorable: Otto." The artist recalls that he used to call her "bewitching elf."

In 1941 she performed in a concert for the closing ceremony of the Venice International Music Festival. In an article in the September 1941 issue of *L'Illustrazione italiana,* Carlo Gatti wrote: "Ildebrando Pizzetti performed five pieces for soprano and orchestra … Mrs. Margherita Carosio sang the pieces wonderfully; truly commendable in the vocal concert music sector and in that for dramatic concert music." The *Gazzetta di Venezia* on 29 September 1941 stated: "Margherita Carosio, with her marvellous voice, fresh and capable of the most sustained modulations, sang the five lyrical pieces with the greatest sensitivity and unrivalled gracefulness."

In the 1942–43 season she sang in both *La Sonnambula* and *Rigoletto* at La Scala. Her debut as Violetta, which remained one of the most important roles in her career, took place in Naples in November 1942 at the Teatro San Carlo. In March 1943 she again performed in *La Traviata,* at the Teatro Reale dell'Opera in Rome. The Safas atelier, in Rome, designed beautiful stage costumes for the singer. The one she wore in the first act was in pink tulle decorated with camellias in the same shade of pink. The artist recalls with regret that the outfit has not survived: "I loved my stage costumes so much… The one I wore in the first act in *Traviata* was really magnificent. I wore it over and over again… but with all those toasts in the first act, with all that champagne… eventually it was covered with stains. I couldn't wear it any more—such a pity! The costume I wore in the second act for Flora's party is fortunately still in good shape, together with its splendid parure made by a Roman manufacturer expressly for me. I have always been happy to wear it, every time I played that role."

The artist was particularly fond of the character of Violetta, as Giacomo Lauri Volpi says in his book *Voci Parallele,* written in 1955. "Margherita Carosio," he wrote, "may be considered a truly extraordinary case. With her the soprano with the lyrical voice surrenders to the singer, to the actress who knows how to and is able to 'walk into' the characters on stage. She does not play the doll or the baby. She is a real woman, with the aura of the everlasting femininity which imbibes her artistry as it throbs in reality. Just observe her in *Traviata,* listen carefully to the modulations of her voice, look at the gestures of her comely figure, the seduction of the chiaroscuros and the execution of the musical design and colours… how can one say she is not a soul that has become a voice and a voice that has become a soul? Reversibility of the spirit in a cycle of melodious enchantment. And look at how Margherita Carosio transforms herself—

ITALFOTO

MARGHERITA CAROSIO
Volchovà Principessa in "Sadkò"
TEATRO DELLA SCALA
STAGIONE LIRICA - ANNO XVI

Margherita Carosio as Princess
Volkhova in Rimsky-Korsakov's
Sadko performed at La Scala
in 1938. The director of stage design
was Nicola Benois, who succeeded
Caramba. The jewels were created
by Corbella.

On the following pages, the necklace
worn by Carosio on this page,
created by Corbella to designs
by Benois in gilt metal and green
and blue crystals. The cross
pendant in gilt metal is adorned
with colourless, green and blue
Bohemian crystals.

Carosio in 1937 at the Teatro Colón in Buenos Aires in the part of Princess Shemakha in Rimsky-Korsakov's *The Golden Cockerel*. She is wearing a costume designed for her by the La Scala atelier. During the same Argentinian tour, Carosio also sang in *Rigoletto, Il Barbiere di Siviglia*, and *Hänsel und Gretel*.

The stage costume created for Carosio for her role as Princess Shemakha at La Scala in Milan, embroidered entirely with multi-coloured crystals and imitation pearls. Corbella itself provided the Bohemian crystals mounted on metal settings to be sewn on the dress, as well as the two large imitation pearls and colourless crystal bracelets the artist would later wear, at La Scala, in *Les Pêcheurs de Perles*.

Gilt earrings designed by Corbella with imitation ruby and diamond crystals modelled by Carosio (together with the necklace on page 70) for her role as Eugenia in Virgilio Mortari's *Il Filosofo di Campagna*, performed in 1938 at Ca' Rezzonico in Venice.

Carosio with Salvatore Baccaloni in the role of Nardo.

Margherita Carosio as Aminta in Richard Strauss' *Die schweigsame Frau*, a new opera for La Scala, performed in 1936, conducted by Gino Marinuzzi, directed by Wallerstein and with scenery and splendid costumes based on the sketches by Cito Filomarino.

through the scenes—into Margherita Gautier, the Lady of the Camellias. In the four acts of the opera, she creates the complete musical and physical character, without restricting herself to the nervous vulnerability in the first act, as usually occurs in coloraturas' performances. Her ingeniousness is versatile, her innate spontaneity of expression and the dualism of nature and spirit are completely combined in this artist. It is not easy to find such a complete personality in the history of opera singing. Nothing extraordinary in her voice—it is true. But her lively sensibility and imagination, supported by an unmistakable awareness and judgement have made Margherita Carosio a singer-actress to whom it would be truly impertinent to ascribe flaws or limitations in her voice."

During the war, in such a highly dramatic period of our history, opera was perhaps one of the only entertainments allowed. The emotions that Margherita Carosio managed to communicate to her audiences did, however, have some negative consequences for her. The artist herself recalls: "One evening there was a high-ranking German officer among the audience who loved opera. At the end of the performance he asked each of the artists to give him a photograph and, to me, he said he wanted one of me as Violetta dedicated to him. I prepared it without thinking of the consequences. How could I refuse? He had been absolutely charmed by my performance, and wanted to be introduced to me. I was called—almost ordered—to his head-

Margherita Carosio

TEATRO ALLA SCALA
MARGHERITA CAROSIO
(Aminta) in " La Donna Silenziosa ,,

CAMUZZI
CRIMELLA

Margherita Carosio

Carosio in the role of Rosina
in Giovanni Paisiello's *Il Barbiere
di Siviglia*, an opera which Maestro
Gino Marinuzzi brought back
on stage for her after almost one
hundred years, performed
at La Scala in the 1938–39 season.

Stage jewels worn by Margherita
Carosio in the role of Rosina.
Created by the Corbella firm, these
were made of imitation pink coral
pâte de verre and silver-plated metal.
Every jewel was signed with the
hallmark "A. Corbella, Milano."

A lovely portrait of Margherita
Carosio as Amina in Bellini's
La Sonnambula.

A Margherita Carosio
esaltata in queste pagine,
a ricordo della nostra
vita artistica, cui
il mondo lirico deve
non poche affermazio-
ni e rivendicazioni
ideali.

Giacomo Lauri - Volpi.
Roma - via A. Bosio 19
Gen. 30 - 1956

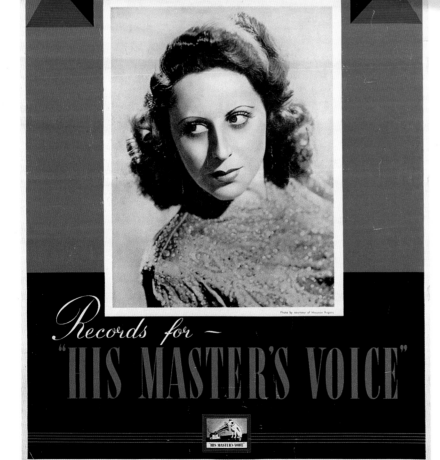

Margherita C

Records for –

"HIS MASTER'S VOICE"

The dedication to Margherita
Carosio written by Giacomo Lauri
Volpi on a copy of the book *Voci
Parallele*, written by the singer
in 1955. The book compares the
most beautiful voices from the 1920s
to the 1950s. Carosio was compared
to Toti dal Monte, the most
important Italian coloratura soprano
of the 1920s and the 1930s.

A poster of "His Master's Voice"
announcing Carosio's recordings.
The legendary tenor Giacomo Lauri
Volpi described the soprano
as "a real singing Sappho."

Top left, Margherita Carosio during
a recording for Italian radio, singing
with tenor Beniamino Gigli.
Top right, with composer Giancarlo
Menotti in 1954, singing a duet
during the rehearsals of Menotti's
Amelia al Ballo, on stage at La Scala.
Bottom, Margherita Carosio
with Maestro Gino Marinuzzi
in a photograph taken during
the interval of Paisiello's *Il Barbiere
di Siviglia*, performed in 1939.

Opposite page, photograph of Tito
Schipa with a dedication to Carosio
in remembrance of a performance
of *L'Elisir d'Amore* they sang together
in Genoa. Bottom, photograph
of Maestro Victor de Sabata
with dedication to Margherita in
remembrance of "their" *Bohème*,
which opened the 1949–50 season
at La Scala, in Milan.

Margherita Carosio

quarters for tea. I remember that when I arrived an attendant took me to a room where the officer was waiting for me. The attendant remained in the room all the time, standing to attention. My host was very kind and congratulated me but, at a certain point he said something that bothered me, 'If all Italian women were like you, Italy would be a great country!' and I retorted, 'You do not know Italian women very well: they are wonderful, much better than me!' And I walked out."

On 6 March 1947, Margherita played Violetta once again in the opening season of the rebuilt La Scala, with a premiere directed by Giorgio Strehler. The artist recalls it was a noisy event. "I had not been very well in that period, suffering from recurrent headaches that forced me to lie down and rest in a dark room. Maestro Tullio Serafin, who was directing the work, was extremely patient and understanding but would not allow anyone to stand in for me. When we were all ready for the premiere, a heated argument started about my work in the past. I was unfairly accused of collaborationism, just like many other great artists who had become famous during the Fascist regime. I was really upset by this: I have always loved my country and the arts, to which I have devoted myself completely." On the evening of the premiere Margherita was very successful. The warm applause of her audience compensated for the campaign against her over the previous weeks.

In the 1947–48 season she sang *L'Elisir d'Amore* at La Scala, with Tito Schipa and in 1948–49 she performed in *Lucia* and *I Puritani* in a gala evening in honour of the President of the Republic.

In 1948, in Bergamo, for the first centenary celebrations of Gaetano Donizetti's death, whose organising committee was led by Bindo Missiroli, Margherita was asked to sing the role of Betly in the comic opera *Betly, ossia la Capanna Svizzera*. The performance was an absolute novelty, more than 100 years since its first performance. Margherita herself gave the cadence to Betly's romance "In questo semplice, modesto asilo." Maestro Franco Capuana was the conductor and Giuseppe Marchioro the director of this opera, which critics declared to be the best blend between the librettist and the composer ever achieved in Donizetti's works. Originally written in one act, in 1936, it was expanded to two acts the year after, when it was scheduled for performance at the Teatro Carolino, in Palermo. Tradition has it that the delightful score was originally written for a company of singers reduced to poverty by the impresario of the Teatro Nuovo in Naples.

TITO SCHIPA

A portrait made by Luxardo, in Rome, depicting Carosio in the first scene of act 2 of *La Traviata*. The magnificent stage costume had been tailor-made for the soprano by Safas, where the famous costumer Umberto Tirelli had just started working.

Earrings with imitation sapphire *pâte de verre* and imitation pearls set in gilt metal, created by Safas, a firm based in Rome, expressly for the costume of act 1 of *La Traviata*, which went on stage at the Teatro dell'Opera in Rome, in 1943, and Margherita Carosio wearing the earrings.

Margherita Carosio

The costume created by Safas in
Rome, for the second scene of act 2
of *La Traviata*. It was a black tulle
dress with sequin-embroidered stars
and decorated with pink camellias.
The set of jewels consisted of a tiara,
a pair of earrings and a necklace.
The bracelets were fastened with two
black velvet ribbons.

Margherita Carosio in 1943.
The singer performed in *La Traviata*
in the opening season of La Scala
reconstructed after the war
(1946–47) under the direction
of Giorgio Strehler, for the first time
at that theatre. E. Gara from *Candido*
wrote: "An angel descended from
heaven: Carosio as Violetta."

Carosio in a stage photograph in the
second scene of act 2 of *La Traviata*.

On the following pages, the parure
made of silver-plated metal
and imitation diamond colourless
crystals.

Margherita Carosio

In November 1948, Carosio sang with the London Symphony Orchestra in a concert at the Royal Albert Hall. The *Daily Mail* reported that her soprano voice had been insured for one hundred thousand pounds. The *Daily Graphic* wrote: "Margherita Carosio, the greatest Italian coloratura soprano, was literally flooded with flowers yesterday at the Royal Albert Hall in London, where she sang with the London Symphony Orchestra and applause broke out repeatedly throughout the concert."

That same year she interpreted a superb *Manon*, by Massenet, and sang *L'Elisir d'Amore* with Tito Schipa at La Scala.

In January 1949, Margherita performed in Venice in *I Puritani*, directed by Tullio Serafin. In that same period, Maria Callas sang in Richard Wagner's *Die Walküre* at La Fenice. A few days before that premiere, Margherita Carosio fell ill with influenza and could not sing in the opera, thus leaving her colleague the chance to play her role. Serafin had been listening to Callas quietly singing an aria in Elvira's role and asked her if she wanted to try. That lucky coincidence changed the course of Maria Callas' career. Within a few days she had sung in both *I Puritani* and *Die Walküre*—a coloratura soprano role and a dramatic soprano role, causing a real stir in the opera world. Carosio recalls an event ten years earlier: in 1939 she had been invited to sing at a concert in Athens, directed by Maestro Issay Dobrowen, whom she had met in Turin where she had sung in *The Golden Cockerel*, for Italian radio, conducted by the same Maestro. After the concert, the soprano Elvira de Hidalgo had gone to congratulate the artist in her dressing room inviting her to her house to listen to a young student—Maria Callas.

In 1949–50 Margherita opened the opera season at La Scala with the performance of *La Bohème*, directed by Giovacchino Forzano and under the baton of Maestro Victor de Sabata. The role required a lyrical soprano voice, and her coloratura soprano voice was not really appreciated by the audience. That same year, however, she returned to La Scala to sing in *I Puritani*—more suited to her singing qualities—and was successful. She also performed

Margherita Carosio signs autographs
on photographs showing her
as Violetta in *La Traviata*.
In the background, a dramatic
portrait of the artist.

In the following pages, Carosio
at the dress rehearsal of the final
scene of Giancarlo Menotti's *Amelia
al Ballo*, performed at La Scala
in 1954. Amelia was the great
soprano's last role at La Scala.

in *Il Campiello*, directed by Nino Sanzogno and in Mozart's *Die Zauberflöte* as Pamina, conducted by Otto Klemperer.

Margherita started suffering from severe headaches and was worried about family problems which made her tired and depressed, a state of mind that was to contribute to her gradual retirement from the stage. In 1952 she was forced to cancel two important roles at La Scala, namely Rosina and Linda. In the issue of 15 May 1952, the monthly magazine *La Scala. Rivista dell'Opera* reported, on page 95: "The illness that has suddenly struck Margherita Carosio has cast a shadow over this godsend of joyfulness—unique, alas, in the world of music. La Scala thought that replacing Carosio with Simionato might mean going back to the original mezzo-soprano Rosina. But no one can think of Rosina without the sparkling coloratura soprano voice—the historic change in the role has been such a blessing. Moreover, Carosio's illness has caused *Linda di Chamounix* to be postponed, and this has been hastily replaced with *Don Pasquale*, directed by Maestro Sanzogno."

Margherita Carosio's last performance at La Scala took place during the 1953–54 season in Giancarlo Menotti's *Amelia al Ballo*, conducted by Maestro Nino Sanzogno.

In the 1950s, she was still a star of international opera. She was very successful at the Liceo de Barcelona where she sang in Donizetti's *Linda di Chamounix*, in *La Sonnambula* and in Massenet's *Manon*.

Margherita Carosio retired definitively from the stage at the end of the 1950s.

Rosanna Carteri

Rosanna Carteri was born in Verona on 14 December 1930. Her mother, who was gifted with a beautiful singing voice, passed on her passion for opera to her daughter, telling her stories from the lives of the great sopranos, right from her early childhood. She was only three years old when she went to a performance of *Aida* at the Arena di Verona. Rosanna was already receiving lessons in voice training and singing from Maestro Cusinati when she started elementary school. Friends of the family included the celebrated soprano Maria Caniglia and her husband, Maestro Donati. It was the voice of Caniglia—her mother used to say—that Rosanna should draw inspiration from. As an adolescent, she studied both singing and piano at the Venice Conservatory.

At the age of fifteen she had the honour of taking part in a concert in the theatre of the small town of Schio, near Vicenza, where the legendary tenor Aureliano Pertile—Arturo Toscanini's favourite opera singer— and the baritone Antenore Reali performed. It was the same Pertile, when introducing her to the public, who said: "Here is to you: the dawn." Pointing to himself he added: "And I am the sunset." In fact the great tenor retired that same year devoting himself to teaching at the Milan Conservatory.

After a tour of concerts in the Veneto region, Carteri won the national competition "Voci Nuove" organised by RAI, the Italian broadcasting corporation. Her official debut in a leading role in the world of opera took place in Rome at the Terme di Caracalla when she played Elsa in Wagner's *Lohengrin*. Carteri was, actually, in Rome to take part in an audition at the Teatro dell'Opera. At the Terme di Caracalla, Renata Tebaldi was playing the part of Elsa in *Lohengrin*. She was supposed to sing in four performances and then run over to Verona for the opening of the Arena's opera season. In fact, the great singer would have been happy to have more time for the rehearsals in Verona, by giving up the last performance. The opera organisers were reluctant to accept Tebaldi's request; however, after Carteri's audition they enthusiastically agreed to Carteri taking her already famous colleague's place. Carteri herself remembers: "The offer left me feeling very enthusiastic, and the risks of singing on such an immense stage as that of the Terme di Caracalla did not cross my mind—standing in for an artist as great and as famous as Renata Tebaldi. In addition to this, I only had two days to prepare, and I was not able to rehearse either with the orchestra or the chorus. I rehearsed with only a piano accompaniment, and then I went on stage. It was an enormous success and, fifteen days later, I was called to San Sebastian, in Spain, for the opening of the opera season. Again in the leading role of *Lohengrin*, once again taking the place of the great Tebaldi, who was unwell. From that moment on, I never stopped."

This first experience on stage also marked the young singer's first encounter with the magical world of costumes and stage jewellery. The jewellery that she wore in Wagner's opera was part of a 1930s collection made by Corbella, consisting of a large belt and a diamond tiara. They had belonged to Maria Caniglia, who gave them to the artist, on that occasion, as a lucky token. Carteri kept these jewels with great affection for the rest of her career.

In that same year, she had her debut on Italian radio, in the role of Alice in *Falstaff*, and played the role of Micaela in *Carmen*, in Trieste.

In 1950 she was seen again in the leading role of *Lohengrin*, for the opening of the opera season at the Teatro Municipale, in Reggio Emilia. In February of that same year she was called to the Teatro dell'Opera in Rome to play the part of Sister Angelica in Puccini's *Trittico*. The critics were enthusiastic; Renzo Rossellini in *Il Messaggero* wrote: "Rosanna Carteri was an exquisite Sister Angelica both in the singing and in the speaking parts. Highly sensitive and well prepared. She will surely succeed in her career."

The daily *Momento Sera* wrote: "Rosanna Carteri is a new voice for our stage. Here is a singer who has the crystal clear voice of youth, extensive and well balanced, and not without a warm expressiveness."

At the Teatro dell'Opera in Rome she also played the part of Liù in *Turandot*. In a column in *Settimana*

Incom one could read: "Liù was Rosanna Carteri, twenty years old, comely and endowed with a very soft voice, and—even more rare—she follows the director's suggestions."

Tebaldi then sang at the Teatro Argentina in Rome in Labroca's *Stabat Mater*, and then in the vocal concert of Martini & Rossi on Italian radio. In May, she went on stage at the Teatro Nuovo in Turin in Gounod's *Faust* and, immediately afterwards, sang in Gaetano Donizetti's *Messa Postuma* at the Teatro San Carlo, in Naples. She was the very first ever to perform in Maestro Ildebrando Pizzetti's *Ifigenia*, on Italian radio.

1951 began with the opening of *Falstaff*, with Carteri in the role of Nannetta at the Teatro Verdi in Trieste. The *Messaggero veneto* wrote on that occasion: "Now impertinent, now coquettish, sweet and delicate, Rosanna Carteri was an ideal Nannetta. This young Veronese soprano continues to attract the attention of the public and critics alike, for the crystal purity of her voice, which is quickly getting stronger."

The same year saw her debut at La Scala in Nicolò Piccinni's *Cecchina o la Buona Figliola* (an opera that had been performed for the first time in Milan nearly two hundred years before, at the Teatro Regio Ducale in 1761, and had never until then been staged at La Scala), conducted by Maestro Franco Capuana and directed by Giorgio Strehler. Critics described her as follows: "Twenty-year-old Rosanna Carteri has a penetrating and melodious voice. She possesses an innocence, entrusting everything to the imagination and not merely to her training." The *Corriere della Sera* reported: "Leading lady Rosanna Carteri is an excellent Cecchina because of her delicate singing and her controlled graceful stage presence."

In March she made her debut at the Teatro San Carlo in Naples as Margherita in *Faust* and at the Teatro Comunale in Bologna in the role of Mimì in *La Bohème*. The critic of *Avvenire d'Italia* wrote: "Carteri, with a pure timbre, a polished and limpid singing, chaste lyricism, a sweet and serene sentimentalism. A future diva of the opera."

For the Maggio Musicale Fiorentino at the Teatro Comunale in Florence she sang Maestro Pizzetti's *Ifigenia*. The Maestro gave the singer a signed photograph with the following dedication: "To Miss Rosanna Carteri, the first and sweetest leading lady of my Ifigenia, with gratitude and all my best wishes."

She then performed in Vivaldi's *Gloria* at the Strasbourg Festival, and, in November, at the Teatro Comunale in Florence, played the role of Sinaide in Rossini's *Mosè* and that of Zerlina in Mozart's *Don Giovanni*.

In January 1952 she performed at the Teatro San Carlo in Naples, in Ottorino Respighi's *Belfagor*. In February she made her debut at the Teatro Massimo in Palermo in the role of Desdemona in Verdi's *Otello*, alongside Ramon Vinay. The young Veronese singer was again at La Scala with *Proserpina e lo Straniero* by the Argentinian Juan Josè Castro, in its first ever performance (that was the winning opera in an international competition to celebrate the 50th anniversary of the death of Giuseppe Verdi), under the direction of Giorgio Strehler. In April she performed in Venice, at La Fenice, in the grand premiere of *I Misteri Gaudiosi*, by Maestro Cattozzo, under the direction of Maestro Vittorio Gui, and stage sets by the painter Giuseppe Cherubini. The monthly magazine *La Scala. Rivista dell'Opera*, issue 31 of 15 May 1952, on page 101, said: "The performance, directed with the affectionate care of Vittorio Gui, was excellent, thanks also to Rosanna Carteri, the sweet, sorrowful and transfigured Maria. The success of *I Misteri Gaudiosi* was enormous. The composer was also warmly congratulated, together with Maestro Gui and all the other performers."

In the same theatre, this time directed by Bruno Walter, she sang Brahms' *German Requiem*, alongside Boris Christoff.

She was chosen by Furtwängler for the role of Desdemona in Verdi's *Otello* at the Salzburg Festival that same year. Wally Reich wrote in *Salzburg Nachtrichten*: "The artist, whose interpretation in the final act was particularly captivating

Carteri as Cecchina (the first from left) in 1951 on the stage of La Scala in Milan, in Nicolò Piccinni's *Cecchina o la Buona Figliola*—an opera which had not been performed for nearly two centuries—together with Silvana Zanolli (Paoluccia) and Tatiana Menotti (Sandrina).

Rosanna Carteri in the role of Elsa in Wagner's *Lohengrin*, in which she made her debut in the world of opera in 1949, at the Terme di Caracalla in Rome.

Rosanna Carteri

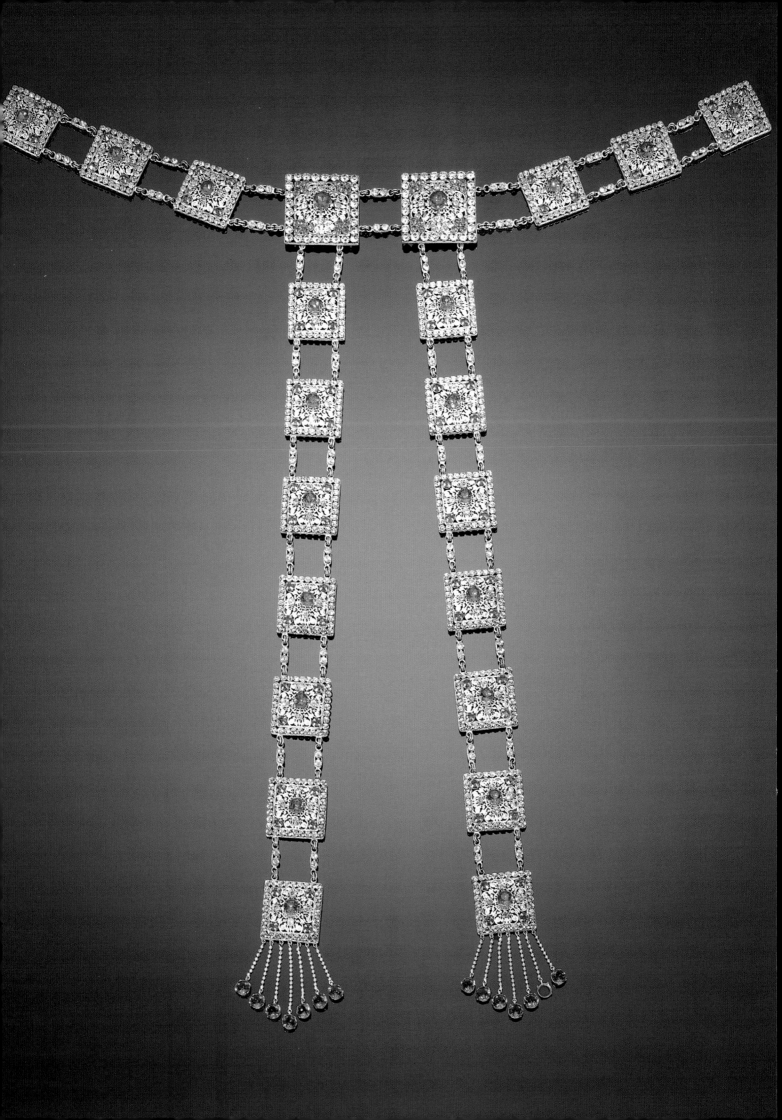

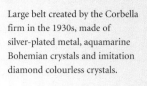

Large belt created by the Corbella firm in the 1930s, made of silver-plated metal, aquamarine Bohemian crystals and imitation diamond colourless crystals.

In the role of Elsa in Richard Wagner's *Lohengrin*.

Carteri (Elsa) on the stage between Giulio Neri (the King) and Gino Penno (Lohengrin).

On page 109, a greeting card for her debut in *Lohengrin* at the Terme di Caracalla sent by soprano Maria Caniglia, who, on that occasion, gave her a set of jewels created by Corbella in the 1930s, which she had worn in various operas during her long career. Below: a dedication by Aureliano Pertile and Antenore Reali, with whom Rosanna Carteri, when she was only fifteen, had made her debut in Schio, near Vicenza.

Roma 13 Luglio 1949

Alla cara Rosanna, perché tutto offrendo all'Arte possa avere dall'Arte i miei stessi successi.
Con l'augurio più af=fettuoso

Maria Caniglia

Lendinara e Schio -

La Signorina Rosanna Carteri alla quale dedico la mia Ammirazione col migliore augurio per la sua carriera possedendo delle ottime qualità canore e musicali e di seguire scrupolosamente tutti gl'Amichevoli consigli studiare - studiare......

Aureliano Pertile

- 6-11-945 -

Alla cara collega Rosanna Carteri tutti i miei auguri e la mia sincera ammirazione,

Antonio Reali

Schio-Lendinara 1945

Carteri in 1952 at the Teatro
Massimo in Palermo, between
director Aldo Mirabella Vassallo
and conductor Oliviero de Fabritiis.

Here she made her debut as
Desdemona in Verdi's *Otello*;
in the role of Otello, Ramon Vinay,
also in the photograph.

Rosanna Carteri

proved, from the first to the last note, to be a 'maestra del Bel Canto'… Her crescendo, her pianissimo… we have hardly ever heard such purity and intensity." On this occasion, Carteri, now famous and much sought after by international theatres, requested the Florentine atelier Cerratelli (which was founded in 1919 on the wishes of baritone Arturo Cerratelli) to create splendid stage costumes and the Marangoni firm of Milan—who were the most popular producers of stage jewellery at the time— to craft a tiara made to her own specifications. The final result (as illustrated on pages 114–15) recaptured the design already made by the Corbella company at the beginning of the century. The pieces of embroidery (illustrated on pages 110–13) were made by the same Marangoni, to complement the tiara.

In December, together with Giuseppe di Stefano at La Scala, she sang in *La Bohème*, directed by the legendary baton of Maestro Victor de Sabata. Teodoro Celli of the *Corriere Lombardo* wrote: "We have admired her in the role of Mimì, for her gentle accent, her youthful vibrant freshness, when she sang

The soprano while rehearsing the scene of the handkerchief with director Aldo Mirabella Vassallo.

Carteri as Desdemona with
the splendid outfit created for her
by atelier Cerratelli in Florence.
The tiara she wore had been crafted
in Ennio Marino Marangoni's
laboratory. The artist herself had
explained to the designer how
she wanted the jewel to be made.

To decorate the dress, Marangoni
provided Cerratelli with gilt metal
elements and Swarovski crystals
in the same style as the tiara.

On pages 114–15, the tiara created
by Ennio Marino Marangoni for
Rosanna-Desdemona, crafted in gilt
metal, imitation pearls and
colourless and light blue, imitation
aquamarine Swarovski crystals.

pieces considered to be the most lyrically detailed in the opera."

Franco Abbiati, of the *Corriere della Sera*, wrote: "Rosanna Carteri, such a timid, sweet Mimì, hopelessly in love, so gentle, has been much admired."

In 1953, at La Fenice, in Venice, she made her debut in Massenet's *Manon* with great success. On 9 February, she sang in the Martini & Rossi concert alongside another legendary name in the world of opera: Beniamino Gigli. In the same month, and again at La Fenice, she appeared in *Delitto e Castigo*, by Maestro Petrollo.

At the Teatro Comunale in Florence, in May, she played Natasha in the world premiere of *War and Peace* by Prokofiev—who died that same year—directed by Maestro Artur Rodzinski. At the end of that year she was once again at La Scala in *Rigoletto* alongside Giuseppe di Stefano and Leonard Warren, under the direction of Nino Sanzogno.

This opera holds a particular place in the artist's memories of her career. "I did not want to accept the role in *Rigoletto*; I thought that the part was not right for my voice. At La Scala, while rehearsing some arias to decide whether or not to accept the role, Maestro Toscanini came in and sat down in the stalls. I did not know him personally, and I was terrified of that legendary character also because I knew how strict he was with singers. The Maestro heard me singing; he then got up and came to the stage to greet me. He sat at the piano and made me sing arias from *Rigoletto* and from *Otello*, and then began to advise me. He told me that I should not be afraid to interpret the part of Gilda, that I had a very rich voice, capable of singing that role and others that, up until then I had always rejected. The great Maestro stayed with me for more than an hour. His advice and precise suggestions persuaded me to accept the role of Gilda. Even though the opera was not very successful, I never regretted that I played the part, as I would always remember it as the occasion when I met Toscanini."

On the evening of the premiere there were protests about the cast, in particular about the tenor and baritone, who were greeted with catcalls, shouts and tomatoes thrown at them. Carteri remembers that she had been warned, in an anonymous letter, that she would be catcalled if she accepted to sing the role in *Rigoletto*. Despite this, she was determined to go on stage. After the uproars of the first night, there were seven more repeat performances without incidents. Carteri also remembers a funny occurrence which

A wonderful Rosanna Carteri in the role of Angelica in Handel's Orlando, *on stage for the Maggio Musicale Fiorentino in 1959, modelling the splendid dress designed for her by Pier Luigi Pizzi.*

happened during a performance: "One night, during act 4—as the script requires—Gilda is stabbed by Sparafucile, put in a sack and taken away. The scene went ahead perfectly. Sparafucile got to the door with me on his shoulders, he should have opened it, but something did not work. From inside the sack I was not able to understand what was happening; I could feel the blows, strange noises, and guessed that the door was blocked. My colleague used all his strength, but all attempts were in vain. I continued to be tossed here and there. After a few minutes, the public followed the scene with interest. At that point my colleague, who continued to pant and swear, whispered to me that he could not force the door open. So, desperate cases call for desperate remedies: I told him to put me down and—trying not to be seen—I got out of the sack and, with all my strength, I helped him open the door. The door finally opened. I got back inside the sack and, finally, Gilda reached backstage. Certainly, for a dead body, I was very lively! From backstage I tried to hear if the audience were laughing. Fortunately they were not. Afterwards, relaxing in my dressing room, I laughed to myself thinking of that moment."

In February 1954, at the Teatro Massimo in Palermo, Carteri played Giulietta in Vincenzo Bellini's *I Capuleti e i Montecchi*. *L'Ora del Popolo* wrote: "An enchanting Giulietta, Rosanna Carteri, is as delicious as ever in every modulation, in every movement on stage, singing with a clear voice, overcoming every arduous passage."

In March, at the Teatro S. Carlos in Lisbon, she sang in Gounod's *Faust*, Menotti's *The Medium* and in the *Le Nozze di Figaro*. The *Seculo* reported: "The other great thing about the performance was Rosanna Carteri, who sang the part of Susanna admirably in the aria 'Deh, vieni, non tardar' and performed beautifully in the recitative, deserving the roaring applause of the public."

The following month, she returned to Rome singing at the Teatro Argentina in Pizzetti's *Ifigenia* and at the Teatro dell'Opera in *La Bohème*. In May, at the Teatro Nuovo, in Turin, she was Desdemona alongside Mario del Monaco in the role of Otello.

At La Scala she played Lucieta in Ermanno Wolf-Ferrari's *I Quattro Rusteghi*. Teodoro Celli of the *Corriere Lombardo* wrote: "Lucieta? Adorable with exquisite manners, able to change from the cunning to the pathetic, full of charm and vocal delicacy, which become the 'bona fia' Rosanna Carteri."

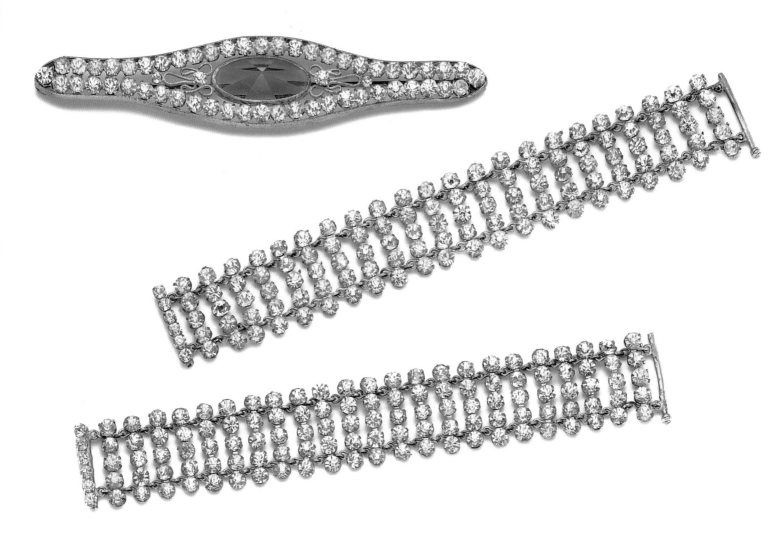

In September she left for California, appearing in San Francisco and Los Angeles in *La Bohème, Manon, Le Nozze di Figaro* and in *L'Osteria Portoghese* (by Cherubini).

In Chicago she played in *La Bohème*. She was given a warm welcome from critics and public alike: they were enthusiastic about the quality of the young soprano's singing and her acting. Marjorie M. Fisher of the *San Francisco News* commented: "Rosanna Carteri is a true star, coming from that small group of stage aristocrats."

On her return from America, she was once again at La Scala where she made her debut in Donizetti's *L'Elisir d'Amore*, with Giuseppe di Stefano, under the direction of Carlo Maria Giulini. She then interpreted the role of Violetta in *La Traviata* on Italian television, which was broadcast on 26 December. Directed by Maestro Nino Sanzogno, Rosanna Carteri was described by Emilio Radius of the *Europeo* as being "a revelation on television… She is fresh and truly beautiful… she was an expressive flower."

In 1955 the artist was the protagonist in two operas by Pietro Mascagni: *L'Amico Fritz*, with Ferruccio Tagliavini, and *Zanetto* with Simionato. In May she returned to La Scala with Mussorgsky's *The Fair at Sorochinsk* and performed again in *Zanetto* under the direction of Maestro Gavazzeni. After the success of *La Traviata* on television, she recorded Massenet's *Manon* for Italian television.

The following year, she worked in the first series titled *Figure del Melodramma*, again for the Italian broadcasting corporation, singing Puccini's romances. With the La Scala company she travelled to South Africa and sang in *L'Elisir d'Amore*. In 1957 she added two more operas composed by Donizetti—*Don Pasquale* and *Linda di Chamounix*—to her repertoire. At the Teatro San Carlo, in Naples, she had the leading role in the premiere of *Vivi* by Maestro Franco Mannino. Then, in August, she left with the La Scala company for Edinburgh, where she sang *L'Elisir d'Amore*.

In 1958, in Naples, she played the role of Magda, in Puccini's *Rondine* at the Teatro San Carlo, winning warm approval. On the occasion of the opening of

A brooch and two bracelets created
by the Corbella firm in the 1930s,
in silver-plated metal and diamond
and topaz imitation crystals.

Rosanna Carteri with Alberto Sordi
during the recording of the film
Mi Permette Babbo?, which also
included the bass Giulio Neri among
the leading actors.

Rosanna Carteri

A picture of Carteri having her hair done by coiffeur Alexandre from Paris, for the grand premiere of Renzo Rossellini's *Il Linguaggio dei Fiori,* which went on stage at the Piccola Scala in Milan in January 1963.

Carteri in a scene of the opera *Vivi* by Maestro Franco Mannino, performed as a grand premiere at the Teatro San Carlo in Naples on 28 March 1957, while dancing with dancer Manovo.

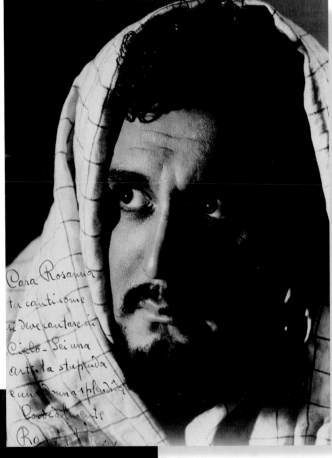

Ramon Vinay in the part of Otello with a dedication to the singer: "Dear Rosanna, you sing the way one must sing in heaven."

Rosanna Carteri in the role of Violetta in Verdi's *La Traviata,* that she would record for RCA in June 1956, with the orchestra and the chorus of the Teatro dell'Opera in Rome, conducted by Pierre Monteux.

Rosanna Carteri

the Maggio Musicale Fiorentino she sang in *La Donna del Lago*, which is the 28th opera composed by Gioacchino Rossini, premiered in Naples on 24 September 1819 and performed again, under the baton of Maestro Tullio Serafin more than a century later at the Teatro della Pergola in Florence. The performers were Rosanna Carteri and Cesare Valletti, who confidently overcame all of the hurdles of a difficult score. Renata Tebaldi and Alberto Sordi were amongst the audience, and, after the performance, went to congratulate Carteri in her dressing room. In October she recorded, for Italian television, a memorable *Otello* with Mario del Monaco. On 7 December 1958, for the opening of the opera season at La Scala, she played Liù in *Turandot* with an exceptional cast including Birgit Nilsson in the role of Turandot and Giuseppe di Stefano in that of Calaf, under the direction of Maestro Antonino Votto. The opening was fondly remembered by the artist: "Usually, people who go to a first night at La Scala, apart from real opera lovers, are those who go because society expects them to, more than out of real enthusiasm. This sort of audience is less likely to let itself be carried away by its feelings. That night, however, maybe because of my enthusiasm or my passion, the usual formal atmosphere was broken. Right from the start I felt that I was in a theatre in South America: the audience gave me a warm standing ovation, something that did not usually happen at La Scala. I continued singing surrounded by that enthusiastic at-

Rosanna Carteri

Maestro Ildebrando Pizzetti's
photograph with a dedication
to Carteri for the grand premiere
of his *Il Calzare d'Argento*
at La Scala, in which the singer
played the role of Metarosa
(on the right) and Giuseppe
di Stefano the part of Giuliano
della Viola.

a Rosanna Carteri, svarissima commovente
Metarosa nella prima esecuzione del Calzare d'argento
al Teatro alla Scala, il 23-3-1961,
riconoscente e grato
Ildebrando Pizzetti

Rosanna Carteri

A smiling Rosanna Carteri in her dressing room after the successful *La Donna del Lago* by Rossini, performed for the first time after more than a century by Maestro Tullio Serafin in 1958 for Maggio Musicale Fiorentino.

Necklace created by Corbella in the 1930s made of silver-plated metal and colourless imitation diamond Bohemian crystals.

On pages 126–27, dress and cloak created by atelier Cerratelli in the late 1950s, in Florence, for Rosanna Carteri's role as Tosca. The jewels were created by Corbella in the 1930s.

mosphere and it was an evening I will never forget." In February 1959 she sang the role of Bianca in Francis Poulenc's *Dialogues des Carmélites*, directed by Margherita Wallmann. She repeated the performance in Palermo at the Teatro Massimo, where she met the author. She later described it as being one the most beautiful roles of her career, and she fondly kept the opera score with the dedication written by the composer: "To the Bianca of my dreams." Subsequently, *Telestar* wrote: "Rosanna Carteri was exceptional in the part of Sister Bianca—who is actually the protagonist of the dialogues—because of her graceful acting, dramatic artistry and her linear way of singing." And the *Giornale di Sicilia* wrote: "Rosanna Carteri was a vibrant and extremely successful Bianca de la Force."

For the Maggio Musicale Fiorentino she sang the role of Angelica in Handel's *Orlando* with beautiful scenery and splendid costumes created by Pier Luigi Pizzi.

In October she got married, in Padua—at the Roman Basilica of San Zeno—to Franco Grosoli, an entrepreneur. The best man was the superintendent of La Scala, Antonio Ghiringhelli. That was the crowning moment of a romance that had blossomed a few months earlier.

In January 1960 she played Desdemona once again with Del Monaco at the Teatro San Carlo in Naples. The critic of *Il Tempo* wrote: "Rosanna Carteri was an ideal Desdemona because of her perfect accents, with her innocent naivety in the first two acts, the dramatic anxiety she created in the third, and the resignation and sorrow in the fourth, where she brought out a purity of singing that only Renata Tebaldi has ever achieved."

In February she sang in *La Traviata*, in Trieste, and in *La Bohème* at Covent Garden in London, in March. When she was expecting her first daughter she decided to leave the stage and started again the following February, when she sang Poulenc's *Gloria*, in a European grand premiere at the Champs-Elysées, under the direction of Maestro Georges Prêtre.

In March she sang at La Scala premiere of Maestro Pizzetti's *Il Calzare d'Argento* in the role of Metarosa, alongside Giuseppe di Stefano, under the direction of Gianandrea Gavazzeni. The daily paper *Il Popolo di Roma* described her as being "a sensitive, passionate Metarosa"; while *Il Resto del Carlino* described her as a "celebrated artist par excellence due to her clear voice and such melodiously grad-

Tiara created by Corbella in the
1930s, made of silver-plated metal
and colourless and aquamarine
Bohemian crystals. On the back
of the central piece is the hallmark
"A. Corbella, Milano." This mark
was used for the first time at the
beginning of the 1900s, but since
in the Corbella family names starting
with an "A" were rather frequent,
this often caused confusion when
dating the objects.

Rosanna Carteri

uated harmonies." *Il Giorno* wrote: "Rosanna Carteri plays Metarosa with clarity and moving expressiveness."

In April she appeared as Alice in *Falstaff* at the Teatro dell'Opera in Rome, in a gala evening in honour of Queen Elizabeth II. For Italian radio she sang in a commemorative concert for the composer Arrigo Boito singing arias from *Mefistofele* and *Nerone*. She also performed in two concerts at the Strasbourg Festival, appearing in Poulenc's *Gloria* in the first, and, in the second, she sang to music of Italian composers, with arias from *La Bohème*, *Tosca*, *I Vespri Siciliani* and *Otello*. It was tremendously successful. *Le Nouvel Alsacien* wrote: "Right from the first note, Rosanna Carteri charmed her audience. She soared straight into the aria. With 'Mi chiamano Mimì' from Puccini's *La Bohème* and with 'L'altra notte in fondo al mar' from Boito's *Mefistofele*, she went straight

to the peak of her career. When with tears in her eyes she sang 'Vissi d'arte' from Puccini's *Tosca* ... only then could one measure her deep feelings for dramatic music. This artist has everything: she is sophisticated, young, attractive, and has great musical sensitivity."

In October she sang in *La Traviata* and *Tosca* at the Opéra in Paris, wearing sumptuous stage costumes created expressly for her by atelier Cerratelli in Florence.

Amongst the greatest successes of 1962, was that of the role of Maureen in Gilbert Bécaud's *Opéra d'Aran* performed at the Champs-Elysées, conducted by Georges Prêtre and directed by Margherita Wallmann. The *Corriere d'informazione* reported: "Last night the audience's opinion was expressed in a long standing ovation ... During the first act only Carteri managed to make the audience applaud in the middle of the

A star-shaped brooch crafted
with colourless and aquamarine
Bohemian crystals created
by Corbella in the 1930s.

The cast of Mozart's *Le Nozze di Figaro* at the Teatro S. Carlos in Lisbon, at the end of the 1954 opera season. In the photograph: Rosanna Carteri, performing the role of Susanna, is next to King Umberto II and Princess Maria Pia di Savoia; among the others, Maestro Oliviero de Fabritiis, Pino Donati, Italo Taglio, Giulietta Simionato and Nicola Filacuridi. King Umberto and Princess Maria Pia went on the stage to congratulate the Italian artists.

In April 1952 Rosanna Carteri
at La Fenice in Venice for the grand
premiere of Maestro Nino Cattozzo's
I Misteri Gaudiosi.

The artist as Desdemona in Verdi's
Otello, in the "Ave Maria" scene,
in the final act. The pink and silver
brocade dressing-gown she is
wearing was created for her by atelier
Cerratelli in Florence.

On page 134, Rosanna Carteri
in the role of Violetta in *La Traviata*,
performed for the Italian television
corporation in 1954. She was
described as "a TV phenomenon."

scene as they were rather circumspect about the *Opéra* by singer-songwriter Bécaud." The *Corriere della Sera* wrote: "Very well rehearsed actor-singers appeared on stage, and Rosanna Carteri gave a magical vocal and stage performance in the role of Maureen." *France Soir* reported: "Rosanna Carteri is one of the most beautiful voices today, and she also possesses an innate sense for the theatre."

In January 1963, Rosanna Carteri performed in another grand premiere in Renzo Rossellini's *Il Linguaggio dei Fiori* at the Piccola Scala in Milan. *La Notte* wrote: "Rosanna Carteri gave Rosita the gift of her vocal talent and her intense dramatic temperament." And, according to *Il Gazzettino*: "The soprano Rosanna Carteri gave a delicate but passionate interpretation of the sorrowful character Rosita, in the gradual transition from being a naive young girl to becoming the tired and deluded adult." The following year the opera would be shown on Italian television.

In March 1965 at the Teatro Verdi, in Padua, she sang in *La Traviata*. *Il Gazzettino* reported: "We will remember her very special way of pronouncing the words 'Amami Alfredo,' beginning with an almost tearful, thread of a voice, letting out an explosion, a little later, the pathos held back with the utmost intensity. And also the famous passage 'Addio del passato,' where the voice alone had the crescendo, leaving the orchestra in the background."

In April 1965 she was once again at the Opéra, in Paris, singing the role of Violetta and reconfirming her clamorous success.

In January 1966 she performed as Desdemona at the Teatro Regio, in Parma. The *Gazzetta di Parma* wrote: "An artist of rare talent and of wonderful richness, Carteri sang at the top of her pure voice with an extraordinary grace, softening the sharp pitch wonderfully, yet again in possession of an exceptional technique."

After these performances Rosanna Carteri was at the height of her success. She decided to interrupt her career to dedicate herself entirely to her family: her husband, her daughter Marina and her son Francesco, born a little earlier. In September 1971 she appeared again in a concert in Parma and, the same month, she sang Rossini's *Stabat Mater* in the Church of the Eremitani, in Padua.

Then, Rosanna Carteri took her leave permanently from her public.

Antonietta Stella

"My very own transistor radio was the present I received from my parents for going up into the first year of middle school. It made me very happy and I kept it in my bedroom. One evening I turned it on and I felt totally ecstatic after listening to a live broadcast from the Teatro dell'Opera in Rome, where Verdi's *Un Ballo in Maschera* with Maria Caniglia and Beniamino Gigli was being performed. It was like 'love at first sight' and, from that moment on, I understood that it would become my passion. I had always had a strong voice; I remember, even as a child, when I sang in the school choir or in church, they always said to me, 'Stella, please, lower your voice!'" This is how Antonietta Stella remembers her first contact with the world of melodrama: "One day, while I was at home singing 'Mi chiamano Mimì' from *La Bohème*, a friend of the family heard me. He was impressed by my voice, and he advised my parents to ask for an audition with Maestro Aldo Zeetti, who had just retired from his career as a conductor and had been appointed a post at the Morlacchi Conservatory in Perugia, where he would devote his time to the teaching of singing. An appointment was made, and the Maestro, seeing that I was so young, asked me kindly, 'So, what would you like to sing?,' thinking that I would choose a song; he was surprised when I replied very confidently, 'Vissi d'arte' from Puccini's *Tosca*. After my rendering the Maestro agreed to help me to perfect my voice and I became his student for four years. When I was nineteen I won the 'Enal' competition in Bologna together with a scholarship. It was the beginning of my singing career."

The springboard for the young Antonietta Stella—who was born in Perugia on 15 March 1929—came in August 1950 in Spoleto, where she made her debut singing the role of Leonora in Verdi's *Il Trovatore*. Her pure, attractive warm voice with a rich mellow Verdian timbre won the public's approval and made her immediately successful. *Il Messaggero* of 12 August reported: "Antonietta Stella's success has made a new star of opera … Antonietta Stella, the dazzling up-and-coming star, excelled in a truly difficult role,

overcoming every obstacle with great confidence. She has, as we predicted, great talent. She performed the dramatic accents wonderfully; her singing expressed unrivalled talent. No one could have ever imagined, if they did not already know, that it was this beautiful young girl's first time on stage. In his operas Verdi forces a 'double genre' on the soprano requiring both dramatic leaps and explosions and virtuoso soprano passages but Antonietta Stella tackled all this confident of her ability. She performed gentle, lyrical and virtuoso passages with the same perfection as the most dramatic ones. She is therefore not only a great performer but also a great singer." In January of the following year she was called to the Teatro dell'Opera in Rome to sing in Verdi's *La Forza del Destino*, for the 50th anniversary of the death of the great Maestro. She sang alongside Mario del Monaco with whom in April she would also sing *Il Trovatore*. Guido Pannain wrote for *Il Tempo* on 28 January 1951: "The Teatro dell'Opera could not have paid Verdi a better tribute than with this young, spiritually rich artist's performance. Antonietta Stella is a priceless performer coming in the name of Verdi to save Italian opera from the mortifying mediocre and hoarse singers leftover from the past. The beauty of her youthful musical style has blown away the cobwebs and brought us joy and solace with her playful, rich, fluid, and unspoilt voice. This is the avenue we ought to follow: remove all the junk, purify the stage." Renzo Rossellini in *Il Messaggero* on 28 January 1951 stated: "Antonietta Stella has passed an extremely demanding test—with distinction. A new young soprano whom we may well describe as being excellently trained, blessed with wonderful talent, not just in her singing, which make her a conscientious and successful performer."

Years later, writing about a concert broadcast by the Italian television corporation Emilio Radius referred to her debut in 1951 in *La Forza del Destino*: "Stella made her debut in Rome in 1951, in a *Forza del Destino* that suits her so well. A brilliant, varied work, full of mystery and richness. The audience and the most astute critics immediately appreciated the young soprano's performance. Everyone is talking about a new Verdian singer, as much sought-after today as in the past; a singer gifted with the variety of talents needed for such a role. Every good debut in a role of Verdi's, incidentally, entails deep research into the problems the celebrated art poses—albeit not fully understood. This is why young singers are always scrutinised by experts of Verdi's operas. Antonietta Stella had something original to say; and she said it in a way that was neither conventional, nor timid. On the contrary she said it very openly, warmly, generously, discreetly but eagerly and with pride. Her dramatic talent was apparent; her operatic qualities were there for all to hear. We should

emphasise why *La Forza del Destino* was not just a fortuitous debut for Antonietta Stella, but an almost predestined one. Could she have made her debut in any of Verdi's other operas? Of course she could! But *La Forza del Destino* suited her better; and she was lucky enough to introduce herself to the public by appearing in this indescribably great, rich, tumultuous melodrama. Only her own modesty prevented her from saying: 'It seems as if it was written especially for me.'"

In Rome she also sang the part of Silvana, in Ottorino

Respighi's *La Fiamma* and the role of Cassandra in Rigacci's *Ecuba*.

Then in Germany she appeared as Amelia in Verdi's *Simon Boccanegra*, an opera that would later be broadcast on Italian radio in November, conducted by Francesco Molinari Pradelli. In December she was in Bologna to perform in another opera by Ottorino Respighi, *Maria Egiziaca*, written in 1932, which had had a successful premiere with Maria Caniglia in the leading role. In January 1952, again at the Teatro dell'Opera, in Rome, Antonietta Stella

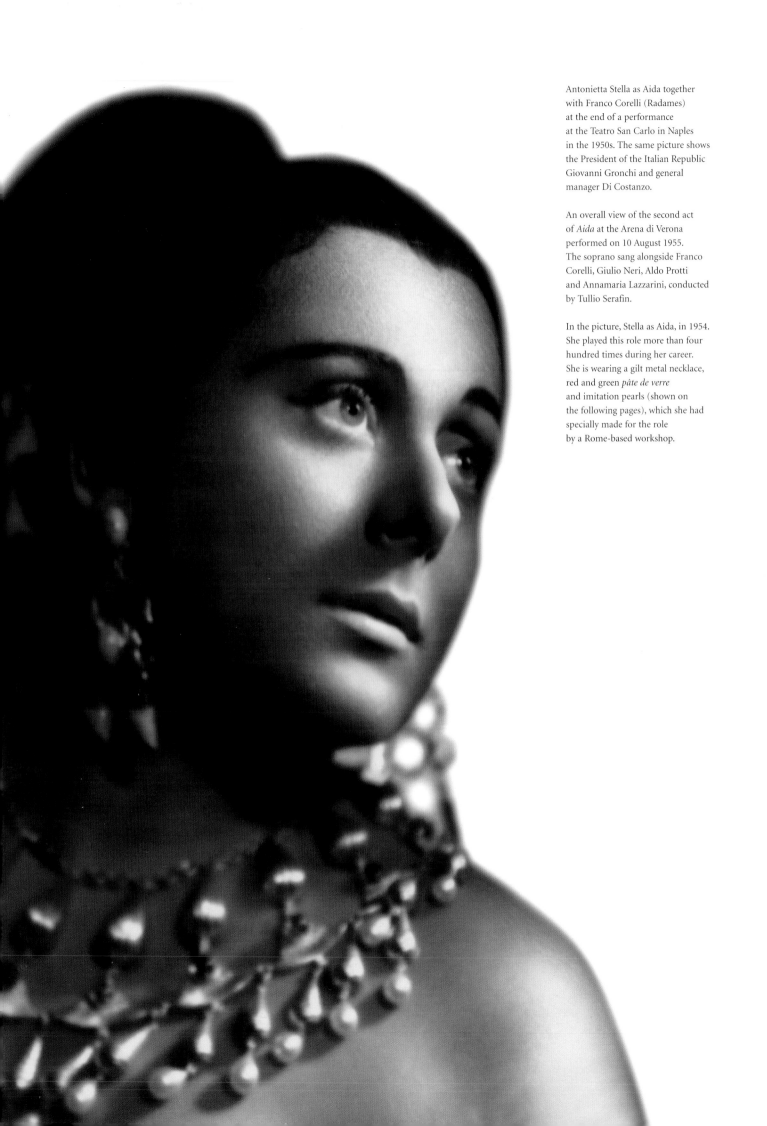

Antonietta Stella as Aida together
with Franco Corelli (Radames)
at the end of a performance
at the Teatro San Carlo in Naples
in the 1950s. The same picture shows
the President of the Italian Republic
Giovanni Gronchi and general
manager Di Costanzo.

An overall view of the second act
of *Aida* at the Arena di Verona
performed on 10 August 1955.
The soprano sang alongside Franco
Corelli, Giulio Neri, Aldo Protti
and Annamaria Lazzarini, conducted
by Tullio Serafin.

In the picture, Stella as Aida, in 1954.
She played this role more than four
hundred times during her career.
She is wearing a gilt metal necklace,
red and green *pâte de verre*
and imitation pearls (shown on
the following pages), which she had
specially made for the role
by a Rome-based workshop.

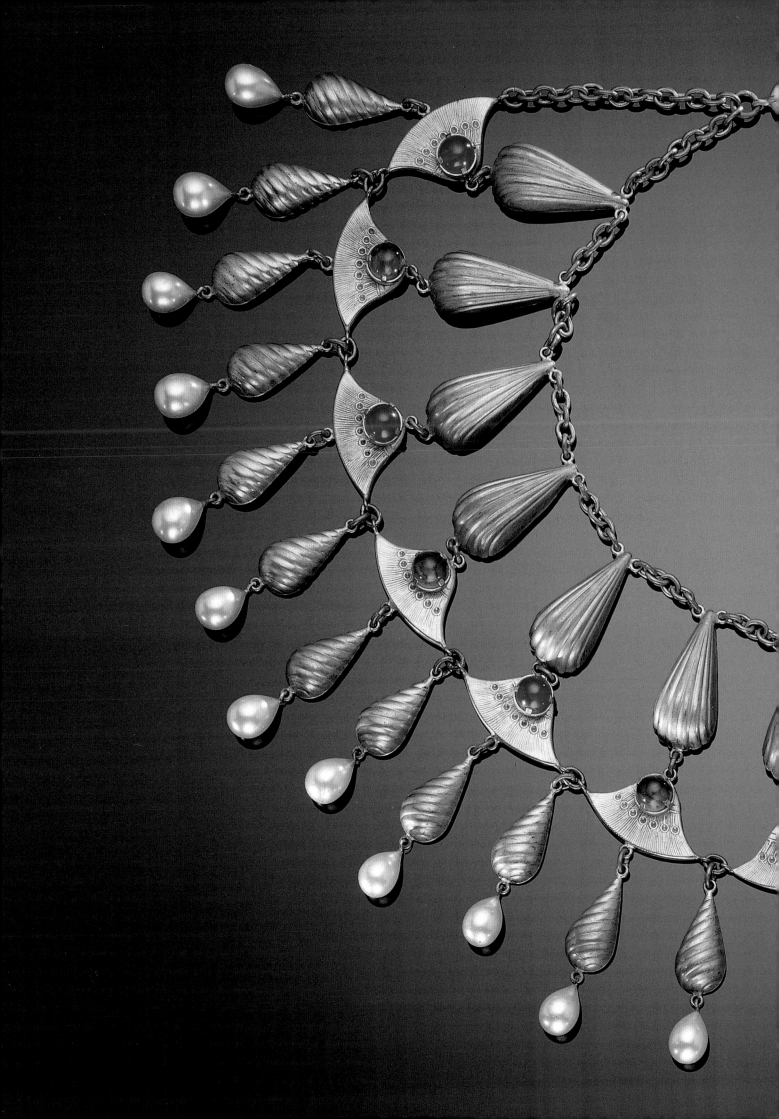

Antonietta Stella

Stella in the role of Mina,
in the centre of an overall
photograph in Giuseppe Verdi's
Aroldo, conducted by Tullio Serafin
at the Maggio Musicale Fiorentino
in 1953.

The singer with Rudolph Bing,
general manager of the Metropolitan
Opera of New York, after performing
Aroldo. Bing was very impressed
by the young artist's singing ability
and he invited her to sing
at the Metropolitan.

Stella at the beginning of her career
with Gino Penno. She is wearing
a gilt metal necklace assembled
with imitation pearls and green
pâte de verre (on the opposite page),
which she would keep in her own
collection and wear for the role
of Adriana in *Adriana Lecouvreur*
by Maestro Francesco Cilea.

Stella as Leonora in Giuseppe Verdi's *La Forza del Destino* with Maestro Dimitri Mitropoulus, who conducted her in Vienna in October 1960.

The singer together with Maestro Tullio Serafin for Giuseppe Verdi's *I Vespri Siciliani*, performed at the Teatro Massimo in Palermo.

Opposite, Antonietta Stella in a dramatic moment of *La Forza del Destino*.

Antonietta Stella

made her debut as the leading lady in *Aida* alongside the great Giacomo Lauri Volpi. It was this role that Antonietta Stella would come to identify with the most, playing it more than four hundred times during her career.

In February at the Teatro Massimo in Palermo, Antonietta Stella played as leading lady in Ottorino Respighi's last work: *Lucrezia*, a posthumous, unfinished opera of the great Maestro, who died on 18 April 1936. In a letter dated 23 April of the same year, his wife Elsa Respighi wrote to her sister-in-law Amelia: "I promise you Amelia, most solemnly, that I will devote myself completely to his work, to the best of my abilities and with all my will, until my very last breath. I examined *Lucrezia* a few days ago: it will be an enormous task to put it together and complete it, but I am certain that he will give me the strength to perform this task to the best of my ability." The pages which were still on the Maestro's piano had been lovingly gathered together by Elsa Respighi the night before his death. According to Maestro De Sabata, once the opera had been put together, it would be almost impossible to distinguish the original pages from the few new ones.

In March, Antonietta Stella was in Lisbon, were she gave her first performance as Desdemona in *Otello*, alongside the celebrated Ramon Vinay, under the direction of Antonino Votto. She sang again in Germany in *Il Trovatore* with Giacomo Lauri Volpi. In January 1953 she sang in the role of Ricke in Franchetti's *Germania*. In March, in Rome, she performed in Guerrini's *Enea*, together with Boris Christoff and Franco Corelli. She then made her debut in Rossini's *Guglielmo Tell* and in Montemezzi's *L'Amore dei Tre Re*.

In Florence, in June Antonietta Stella found herself the subject of the admiration of Rudolph Bing, from the Metropolitan Opera of New York. She played the part of Mina in Verdi's *Aroldo*, under the direction of Tullio Serafin. The general manager of the New York theatre was very impressed by Stella's performance and he asked her to sing at the Metropolitan in the future.

From July to August of that year she was at the Arena

Verdi's *Trovatore* opened the 1962–63
opera season at La Scala in Milan.
The cast were Antonietta Stella
(Leonora), Franco Corelli (Manrico),
Ettore Bastianini (the Count
of Luna) and Fiorenza Cossotto
(Azucena), conducted by Maestro
Gianandrea Gavazzeni and directed
by Giorgio de Lullo; stage and
costume designer was Pier Luigi
Pizzi who, in the picture, is putting
the finishing touches to the soprano's
costume.

Stella between Franco Corelli
and director De Lullo.

Antonietta Stella with Ettore
Bastianini. During the grand
premiere, from the gallery, someone
shouted: "You are Verdi's soul!"

Antonietta Stella

Antonietta Stella and Giuseppe di Stefano, smiling happily after the successful premiere of Verdi's *Luisa Miller* at the Teatro Massimo in Palermo in January 1963.

Group photograph after the premiere. On Stella's left, director Margherita Wallmann, Maestro Nino Sanzogno and stage designer Pier Luigi Pizzi; on her right, tenor Giuseppe di Stefano.

Antonietta Stella

Antonietta Stella as Cio-Cio-San
in Giacomo Puccini's *Madama
Butterfly*, performed at the
Metropolitan Opera, in New York,
conducted by Maestro Dimitri
Mitropoulus.

A poster of the Teatro dell'Opera,
in Rome, bearing the notice "Sold-out."

Antonietta Stella

Antonietta Stella as Floria Tosca
in Giacomo Puccini's *Tosca*.
She is wearing a tiara in silver-plated
metal and Swarovski crystals
(on the opposite page) which she
commissioned specially for this role
from a Rome-based firm.

On page 154, Stella with director
Margherita Wallmann during
the rehearsals of Giuseppe Verdi's
La Battaglia di Legnano which,
on 7 December, opened the 1961–62
opera season at La Scala in Milan.

On page 155, the soprano as Lida
on the evening of the premiere
of *La Battaglia di Legnano*
at La Scala; together with Maestro
Gianandrea Gavazzeni, baritone
Ettore Bastianini and director
Margherita Wallmann during
the rehearsals.

Antonietta Stella

di Verona with performances from *Il Trovatore* and *La Forza del Destino* and, in December, in Rome at the Teatro dell'Opera as Alice in Verdi's *Falstaff* with Mariano Stabile.

Her debut at La Scala in Milan took place in 1954 with *Otello*, alongside Mario del Monaco and Tito Gobbi. In September she was in Rio de Janeiro, where she sang in *Simon Boccanegra* and *Il Trovatore*. In March 1955 she performed in *Un Ballo in Maschera* at the Teatro dell'Opera in Rome with Giuseppe di Stefano, and in May in *I Vespri Siciliani* in Turin.

In September, Stella recorded *La Traviata* for the record company His Master's Voice at La Scala, directed by Tullio Serafin. The Maestro, who was a great admirer of hers, wrote on the score, on 21 September 1955: "To Madame Antonietta Stella who has nothing to fear from Violetta. Everyone who has heard and admired her can praise her extremely rare talents: an exquisite singer, a sensitive artist. I can also add my own personal acknowledgement: a music lover, a diligent student (she completed the performance and interpretation of this difficult, amongst the most difficult melodramatic characters, in little

more than a week, and the result may be judged by all who listen to this recording), inspired by this enthusiasm, with such willpower to reach the top that she will make it. With my kindest affection, Tullio Serafin."

In October 1955 she recorded Umberto Giordano's *Andrea Chénier* for Italian television with Mario del Monaco. That same month she went to Rio de Janeiro, were she sang the role of Ilara in Gomes' *Lo Schiavo*. In February 1956 again at La Scala she performed in Mozart's *Don Giovanni*, singing the part of Donna Anna, with Elisabeth Schwarzkopf and Rosanna Carteri. Antonietta was now a top singer; she was able to enter the world of opera at a time when it was dominated by the likes of two great divas: Renata Tebaldi and Maria Callas. In April 1956 at La Scala, the soprano had the lead role in Verdi's *Un Ballo in Maschera*, directed by Maestro Gianandrea Gavazzeni, her great admirer, who admitted that he appreciated her for her rich and beautiful Verdian voice, more than for her exceptional stage presence.

In high demand from all the international theatres,

Picture with dedication by Maestro Tullio Serafin to Antonietta Stella.

Stella as Amelia in March 1956 at the Teatro San Carlo in Naples, in a photograph which shows her joking with her colleagues Giuseppe Taddei and Ferruccio Tagliavini after a performance of Verdi's *Un Ballo in Maschera*.

Necklace and earrings made of gilt metal, green *pâte de verre*, colourless and green Bohemian crystals created by the Corbella firm in the 1930s.

On page 158, Antonietta Stella in a photograph taken on 9 December 1965 at the Teatro Massimo in Palermo in the role of Elvira in Giuseppe Verdi's *Ernani*. From the left, singers Limarilli and McNeill, Maestro Nino Sanzogno, Raffaele Ariè and director Mario Bolognini.

On page 159, silver-plated earrings with Swarovski crystals and imitation pearls, which Stella had made by a Rome-based workshop in the 1950s, which she later wore in several operas.

Antonietta Stella

in July she went to Buenos Aires to sing in *Aida* and, in August, to Rio de Janeiro to perform in the leading role of Vincenzo Bellini's *Norma*, alongside Mario del Monaco and Elena Nicolai, and she also performed in *Aida*. In September and October she was in Japan, to sing in *Aida* and *Tosca*; in November, engaged by Rudolph Bing, she sang *Aida* and *Il Trovatore* at the Metropolitan Opera in New York. The American critics were unanimous in praising Stella's warm, ample, wonderful voice and her ability to plunge into the roles she played.

On December 7 she was at La Scala for her first opening of the season at that theatre, performing in the role she was most fond of: Aida, under the direction of Antonino Votto and with Giuseppe di Stefano.

At the beginning of 1957, Stella performed at the Teatro Massimo, in Palermo, singing the part of Elena from *I Vespri Siciliani*, conducted by Tullio Serafin. In February she returned to New York to appear in *Tosca*, alongside Gianni Poggi and under the direction of Dimitri Mitropoulus. In March she was in Philadelphia, singing in *Il Trovatore* and in New York, in *Don Carlos*. In April she was once again at La Scala, where she performed *La Forza del Destino* with Di Stefano. At the Arena di Verona she played Mimì in

La Bohème, once again alongside Giuseppe di Stefano, and in November she was back at the Metropolitan Opera, where she sang *Tosca* and made her debut as Violetta in *La Traviata*. The year ended with *Il Trovatore* at the Teatro San Carlo in Naples, and on 7 December, at the same venue, Stella sang in *Linda di Chamounix*.

1958 saw her in the leading female role in an exceptional event in New York's Metropolitan Opera: a performance of Puccini's *Madama Butterfly*, conducted by Dimitri Mitropoulus. For this production Rudolph Bing had organised a whole new staging of the opera, summoning the director and scenery designer from Japan, to recreate the authentic atmosphere of *Madama Butterfly*, making it very Japanese, and in particular to give life to a Cio-Cio-San, making her move, sigh and suffer like a Japanese woman. In order to finance such an expensive production, Rudolph Bing found a patron in Cornelius V. Starr and, to play the role of Madama Butterfly, the general manager called the great Antonietta Stella.

Hedy A. Giusti, writing in the *Corriere d'informazione*, evening edition of 19–20 March 1958, interviewed the singer in her dressing room, described as being full of flowers and pages from the New York daily papers and magazines whose headlines reported Stella's roaring success. "Nothing short of amazing, can describe the enthusiastic musical atmosphere of this exceptional performance, creating a real sensation. And 'our, good old *Butterfly*' has created a real sensation, moved our parents and grandparents, and all of us … Motohiro Nagasaka, stage designer, and Yoshio Aoyama, director, came to New York to work with scenes and performers. The result is an authentic *Butterfly*, stirring in every way and of a beauty without equal. We spoke to Antonietta Stella, the incomparable new Butterfly. She did not say anything but we noticed that she had lost a lot of weight. 'No, it is not the American food,' she said, 'it's the Japanese. I had to work for three weeks from ten until five, practically non-stop. And when I say work, I mean work. Every movement of every finger had to be under control, every movement of the head had a meaning, every gesture had to be in harmony. It was only my feet that I did not need to think about, for throughout most of the opera I have to kneel. By the end of rehearsals

On the opposite page, two dramatic images of Antonietta Stella in the role of Adriana during the final scene of *Adriana Lecouvreur*, performed in Bologna in March 1966.

Stella as Elisabetta in the Viennese production of Giuseppe Verdi's *Don Carlos*.

I couldn't sit or stand any more. Just think, that at a cocktail party given by Mr. Starr in my honour, I had to excuse myself because I needed to rest for a moment; that is, I felt I had to keel down. My muscles could not hold me up in any other position. But kneeling down is nothing—getting up is hard! According to the Japanese, a woman should get up like a butterfly, leaving the ground, harmoniously and without showing any effort. But it was worth suffering! Oh, yes, it was all really worth it!"

In fact both public and critics received Antonietta Stella's performance enthusiastically. Bold headlines in the entertainment pages of the New York dailies ran: "Miss Stella in the new *Madama Butterfly* is much more than just a singer and an actress, she is Cio-Cio-San." Hedy A. Giusti wrote in his article, in the *Corriere d'informazione*: "We have nothing to add—we have never seen Miss Stella reach such artistic heights: her singing and gestures were all in harmony, and never, not even for one moment, does one get the impression of any physical effort. Her great melodious voice is richly expressive and, in the role of Butterfly, she has given us everything."

This *Butterfly* will go down in the history of the Metropolitan Opera as the most beautiful ever. Stella-Butterfly then went on tour in the major cities of the United States. In July Antonietta Stella was in Buenos Aires to perform in *Otello*, with Ramon Vinay and then to Rome with *Aida* and *Tosca*. At the Arena di Verona she sang *Aida* in August, and then toured Mexico, ending the year at the Teatro San Carlo in Naples with *Andrea Chénier*, with Franco Corelli and Ettore Bastianini.

In 1959 Stella was back at the New York Metropolitan Opera, and later returned to Rome, to the Teatro dell'Opera, where she sang *La Traviata*; then to Palermo in April, where she made her debut in Puccini's *Manon Lescaut*. In the same month of April, at La Scala, she sang the role of Sister Angelica, directed by Gavazzeni. Stella then travelled again to the United States after performing in Rome and Vienna. She ended the year at the Teatro dell'Opera, in Rome, with a splendid *Un Ballo in Maschera* alongside Giuseppe di Stefano and Ettore Bastianini.

In 1960 Antonietta Stella performed in Rome in Catalani's *Wally*. Then she left again for the United

Antonietta Stella in the role
of Princess Fedora Ramazov in
Umberto Giordano's *Fedora* at the
Turin's Teatro Regio in May 1967.
She is wearing the tiara created in
1939 by the Corbella firm in Milan
for mezzo-soprano Gianna
Pederzini, who, that year, played
the same role at La Scala. It was
Pederzini herself, an admirer
of the singer Stella, who gave her
this tiara and the cross-shaped
pendant (shown on page 45)
as a good-luck token.

The gilt metal tiara with colourless
and green Bohemian crystals
and imitation pearls. On the back,
in the centre of the piece, there is
the hallmark "A. Corbella, Milano."

A 1950s photograph portraying
Stella during one of her visits
to New York and, in the background,
the wonderful Stella in the role
of Amelia in *Un Ballo in Maschera*.

On page 167, Antonietta Stella
in *Adriana Lecouvreur*.

States and, eventually, in April, returned to Milan to La Scala for Verdi's *Un Ballo in Maschera*, conducted by Gavazzeni. Once again to Vienna, and then finishing in Milan in December with *Don Carlos*.

1961 opens with *La Forza del Destino* at La Scala and closes, at the same theatre, with Stella's second opening on 7 December, performing Verdi's *La Battaglia di Legnano* in the role of Lida alongside Franco Corelli and Ettore Bastianini, conducted by Maestro Gianandrea Gavazzeni. In October Stella was in Berlin to perform in Verdi's *Requiem Mass* directed by Herbert von Karajan.

Verdi's *La Battaglia di Legnano* was chosen for the closing of the celebrations for the Unity of Italy. On 8 December 1961 Franco Abbiati wrote in *Corriere della Sera*: "All in all, the artistic results displayed an unusual dignity and excellence, in particular with reference to the strictly musical aspect of the performance, which saw Gavazzeni, as a lively—albeit cautious—performer … Moreover, it was Antonietta Stella, the magnificent Lida, who brought out the character in her canto, with delightful inflections and graceful flourishes."

The following year on 7 December, at La Scala, Stella was once again the leading lady in the opening of the 1962–63 opera season with Giuseppe Verdi's *Il Trovatore*, alongside Franco Corelli, Ettore Bastianini, Fiorenza Cossotto, under the direction of Gianandrea Gavazzeni, with stage design and costumes based on designs by Pier Luigi Pizzi. The newspapers of the day reported that during the interval the audience talked about Stella's elegance, not only because of the beautiful costumes that Pier Luigi Pizzi had created expressly for the artist, but in particular for her magnificent voice and stage presence. In fact, the *Corriere della Sera* of 8 December 1962 wrote that, from the gallery, admirers called out: "You are Verdi's soul!"

In January 1963 at the Teatro Massimo in Palermo, Stella performed in Verdi's *Luisa Miller* alongside Di Stefano, conductor Maestro Sanzogno. In that year she sang in the best Italian theatres and, from June to September, she was in Vienna where she performed a repertoire of Verdi's works including *La Forza del Destino*. The soprano then went to Tokyo in October, with *Il Trovatore* and, in December, she made her debut in the role of Selica in Meyerbeer's *L'Africaine* at the Teatro San Carlo in Naples. The following year Stella performed again in a vast repertoire all over Europe and, in March 1966, made her debut in Bologna in the leading role in *Adriana Lecouvreur*, an opera she was to sing in all Italy's best

theatres that year. In 1967 she sang *Il Trovatore* on Italian radio alongside Carlo Bergonzi directed by Maestro Basile and, in May, she premiered in Turin, in Umberto Giordano's *Fedora*.

The mezzo-soprano Gianna Pederzini was sitting among the audience; she had sung the same role at La Scala in Milan many years before, in 1939, before the composer himself. The artist was so impressed and moved by Stella's performance that afterwards she ran to her dressing room to congratulate her. She also told Antonietta Stella that she wanted to give the original stage jewellery—expressly made for her for that opera and which she really loved—only to her. These were splendid jewels, crafted by Corbella, among which there was a large decorative headdress of typical Russian *kokoshnik* style. The next day, as promised, Pederzini gave Stella this historic stage jewellery, which the soprano wore for all her successive performances, keeping them forever with fond memories of the great artist and the great success she achieved. She would be seen interpreting this role again in February of the following year at the Teatro dell'Opera in Rome, alongside Mario del Monaco. In December at the Teatro San Carlo in Naples, she sang the role of Poppea in Monteverdi's *L'Incoronazione di Poppea*. In 1969 she was the protagonist, on Italian radio, in Maestro Riccardo Zandonai's *Conchita*. In the 1970s Stella added other important characters to her repertoire: Irmengarda in Gaspare Spontini's *Agnese di Hohenstaufen*, under the direction of Maestro Riccardo Muti, Euridice in Gluck's *Orfeo ed Euridice*, under the direction of Maestro Ozawa, and Odabella in *Attila* by Verdi, Maestro Riccardo Muti conducting. Stella played the leading role in Gargiulo's *Maria Antonietta*, an opera she would perform in 1973 at the Teatro dell'Opera in Rome, under the direction of Maestro Urbini; in April 1974 she sang the leading part in De Bellis' *Maria Stuart* at the Teatro San Carlo in Naples.

Many years have passed since her debut in August 1950. Antonietta Stella decided to retire from the stage to devote herself entirely to teaching young singers her art.

Renata Tebaldi

"Hindering the career of such a voice would be a mistake, almost a crime, I would say." That's what Maestro Riccardo Zandonai, director of the Conservatory of Pesaro, told Mrs. Tebaldi after young Renata sang the aria "Ebben ne andrò lontana" from Catalani's *Wally*. And then added: "Voices like your daughter's may be found once or twice a century."

The great Maestro was proven right. There has never been a more splendid, rich and stirring voice than Renata Tebaldi's. It is equally pure across the whole range, capable of softening to sweet and clear tones.

Renata Tebaldi was born on 1 February 1922, in Pesaro. At seventeen, she started singing lessons with Maestro Ettore Campogalliani at the Parma Conservatory, where she had already attended piano classes. But it was the great singer Carmen Melis who appreciated Renata's potential and helped her in defining her vocal timbre and colour. Tebaldi first appeared on stage on 23 May 1944 at the Teatro Sociale, in Rovigo, playing the role of Elena in Arrigo Boito's *Mefistofele*, under the direction of Giuseppe del Campo. The *Quotidiano di Rovigo* reported the next day: "Renata Tebaldi, one of the great Carmen Melis' young students, made her debut in the difficult role of Elena. No premiere could ever have been better. Renata Tebaldi is gifted with vocal and acting qualities and the sincere and warm applause she received surely marks the beginning of a brilliant career."

In January of the following year, she made her debut as Mimì, in *La Bohème*, at Parma's Teatro Ducale. In that city Tebaldi also sang the part of Suzanne in Mascagni's *L'Amico Fritz* and Giordano's *Andrea Chénier*. In Trieste, on 30 December, she performed for the first time in a role which was to become her hallmark: Desdemona in Verdi's *Otello*. In January 1946, in Richard Wagner's *Lohengrin*, she played Elsa for the first time.

That same year she had an audition with Maestro Toscanini in Milan, when he returned from the United States for the grand opening of the renovat-ed La Scala. Tebaldi recalls that the audition had been scheduled for 10 o'clock and, in order to calm her nerves about that decisive meeting she decided to leave her home in Via Broggi at 8 o'clock and have a long walk. When she walked into La Scala she was escorted to the well-known Sala Gialla—the audition hall. The Maestro was sitting there together with his son Walter, Mr. Ghiringhelli (the general manager of the theatre), and another gentleman. After the usual questions, Renata sang the aria "La mamma morta," from *Andrea Chénier*. When she had finished, the Maestro asked her if she had prepared anything else and she replied: "The 'Ave Maria,' from Verdi's *Otello*. She started from the "Canzone del salice" and at that point Toscanini began beating time with his hand. Renata immediately followed the Maestro, but the pianist, who had his back to the audience, thought the singer was out of time and started staring and frowning at her. The soprano, in turn, glowered at him trying to make him understand that he should look at the Maestro. Eventually, the pianist understood and very discreetly looked over his shoulder a bit so he could follow the rhythm the Maestro was beating. At the end of the piece, Toscanini exclaimed: "Brava, brava!"

This is how the young singer came to be chosen by Arturo Toscanini for the great post-war music event. On 11 May 1946, La Scala in Milan reopened its doors, celebrating its resurrection from the ashes of war. The young artist sang the "Preghiera" from Rossini's *Mosè* and was the soloist in Verdi's *Te Deum*. It was after this concert that the famous Maestro gave her the nickname of 'Angel's Voice.'

The soprano became very popular thanks to this event, that was broadcast worldwide.

In May, again in Milan, Tebaldi sang at the Teatro Lirico in *Andrea Chénier* and, in July, in *Mefistofele* as Elena. In August, she performed at the Palazzo dello Sport—the summer venue of La Scala—and, between July and September she sang in *Lohengrin* and in *Mefistofele*, in the main role as Margherita. She fondly recalls the event. "As I was rehearsing at the Palazzo dello Sport, I could see a gentleman in the distance who kept on changing seats; from the central stalls, he moved to the side and then went up the steps all the way to the top. I couldn't understand what he was doing and was really intrigued by that strange person and asked who he was. 'Maestro Toscanini,' they told me. He was there to make sure that my voice reached every point of the auditorium."

In October, she made another debut, performing as Tosca this time at the Teatro Bellini, in Catania. On 20 December 1946, she sang at La Scala for a special charity event for the poor children of Milan. At that concert, directed by Tullio Serafin, Tebaldi performed alongside Giuseppe Malipiero and Cesare Siepi.

In 1947, Tebaldi sang first in *Die Meistersinger von Nürnberg*, directed by Tullio Serafin, and then in *La Bohème*.

In August of that year, Renata Tebaldi was at the Arena di Verona where she played Margherita in *Faust*, again directed by Maestro Tullio Serafin. On 4 August 1947, G. Bertolasa wrote in *Il Nuovo Adige*: "Renata Tebaldi has a bright, effortless well-trained voice, a beautiful timbre. Her voice seduces and captivates, a vibrant flowering of enchanting joyful youth. A truly lyrical and sentimental Margherita, she was tender and affectionate in her first meeting with Faust as shown in her superbly phrased 'Aria dei gioielli,' full of intensity and passion in the love duet, when her voice was fully extended, and full of sorrow in the prison scene."

That same year, she made a debut as Violetta in *La Traviata* performing at the Teatro Bellini, in Catania. She opened the 1948 season at La Fenice, in Venice, with the same opera, under the baton of Maestro Serafin.

In April 1948, she performed for the first time in the role of Elisabeth, in Wagner's *Tannhäuser*, under the direction of Maestro Karl Böhm, who a few years later said that Renata Tebaldi was the best Elisabeth he had directed in his whole career. The young artist made another debut, the same month, in Casavola's *Salammbô* at the Teatro dell'Opera in Rome and as Elsa in Wagner's *Lohengrin*, for the Maggio Musicale Fiorentino.

On 21 September, Renata Tebaldi performed in *Andrea Chénier* at La Scala. The review *Tempo di Milano* reported: "The superb stage performance of soprano Renata Tebaldi is worthy of mention. Her voice, her intelligence and dramatic power have produced a marvellous Maddalena di Coigny. She

received a thunderous ovation." In December, Margherita was back again at La Scala performing in Gounod's *Faust*, directed by Maestro Antonino Votto.

In February 1949, in a gala evening at La Scala she played Desdemona in Verdi's *Otello*, with Ramon Vinay, directed by Maestro Victor de Sabata. The *Corriere della Sera* of 6 February 1949 wrote: "Renata Tebaldi, a magnificent Desdemona, sang with a sweet, soft and clear voice; always gentle and in love. She was particularly moving in two jewels such as the 'Canzone del salice' and 'Preghiera a Maria.'"

In March, again at La Scala and again under De Sabata, Tebaldi sang in *Andrea Chénier* to commemorate Umberto Giordano, while in Lisbon, at the Teatro S. Carlos, she played the role of Donna Elvira in Mozart's *Don Giovanni*, and of Alice in *Falstaff*.

Tebaldi made her debut as Pamira in Gioacchino Rossini's *L'Assedio di Corinto*, during the Maggio Musicale Fiorentino. Leonardo Pinzauti wrote in the daily *Il Mattino* of 5 June 1949: "Soprano Renata Tebaldi stands out. Her voice—with its inner vibrations—draws expressiveness from its timbre, with no contractions, not even in the more dramatic passages. And this is without mentioning her commanding stage presence. She received repeated curtain calls."

In January 1959, she was at La Scala in *Falstaff*, directed by Maestro Victor de Sabata. La Scala had requested the young artist to sing the role of Aida. The soprano hesitated for fear that her voice was not suitable for the part. The theatre manager, knowing how much Tebaldi admired Maestro Toscanini, asked the Maestro himself to persuade her to accept the role—which everyone thought was just perfect for the young singer. Tebaldi vividly remembers the emotion she felt when she received the Maestro's invitation, and will never forget the day she went to visit him at his home in Via Durini. Toscanini received her in his study, sat down at the piano and accompanied her in the arias of Aida, starting with the last act, going all the way back to the first. The great Maestro's advice will remain impressed on her memory: "I know why you are hesitating. You are worried about the recitative and 'Ritorna vincitor.' You feel happier in the second and third acts."

That is exactly how the soprano felt. The Maestro continued: "It is an opera made for you. Aida is not an impetuous and passionate woman: she is sweet.

Until now that role has never been interpreted as Verdi wrote it. Everyone insists in expressing a dramatic intensity by singing it 'forte' and 'agitato.' What is needed is nostalgia and expression! If you capture that, you will sing the part of Aida as it should be sung." The young singer treasured this advice and as the tenor Giacomo Lauri Volpi wrote in *Voci Parallele*: "Tebaldi in Aida, loses herself in the role, smothering for an instance all of her inner turmoil when she sings 'In estasi beate, la terra scorderem'—with that 'beate,' that miraculous 'e,' so full of insight…"

In February, La Scala added *Aida* to its programme, expressly for Tebaldi. In the evening of 12 February she made her debut with Mario Del Monaco, under the direction of Maestro Antonino Votto. It was the first of seven performances, and received a wild ovation.

Young Tebaldi photographed next to the general manager of the Teatro San Carlo, Di Costanzo, and the cast of Gounod's *Faust* which went on stage at Villa Floridiana, in Naples.

The *Tribuna di Milano* of 13 February 1959 reported: "A quintet of beautiful voices was on stage, starting with Renata Tebaldi. Her warm character and the delicate blend of her softly resonant voice made her emphasise the lyrical passages more than the dramatic ones. She was an extremely sophisticated and stirring performer of the third act romance 'O cieli azzurri,' singing tenderly in the love duet passages, and with a melodious desperation in the final duet." Three unscheduled performances were added, but Tebaldi honoured a commitment she had with the Opera House in Lisbon and was therefore replaced by Maria Callas, who made her debut at La Scala in Milan on that very occasion.

That same year, during the Maggio Musicale Fiorentino, she sang in Gaspare Spontini's *Olimpia*, directed by Maestro Tullio Serafin. Leonardo

Renata Tebaldi in the role
of Elisabeth, in Wagner's *Tannhäuser*
at the Teatro San Carlo, in Naples,
in April 1948.

Crown designed by the Corbella firm
in the 1930s and worn by Renata
Tebaldi in *Tannhäuser*. It was made
of silver-plated metal, colourless
Bohemian crystal and *pâte de verre*
imitation turquoise, imitation pearls.
The parure included a large belt and
cloak clasps, shown on the next
pages.

On page 174, Renata Tebaldi is
portrayed with Maestro Karl Böhm
during the interval of *Tannhäuser*,
wearing the complete parure,
and in her dressing room, as he
congratulates her. Years later, in
an interview, Karl Böhm said Tebaldi
was the best Elisabeth he had ever
directed.

On page 175, the large belt and
the cloak clasps created by Corbella
in the 1930s which form a parure
together with the crown on page 173.

Pinzauti wrote in *Il Mattino* on 15 May 1959: "Renata Tebaldi (Olimpia), fascinating and comely, sang with the sweet expressiveness that her voice conveys even in the most dramatic passages." Teodoro Celli wrote in the *Corriere Lombardo*, the same day: "The best performer was Renata Tebaldi, her vocal style the purest."

In June she sang at La Scala for three important debuts: on the 9th in Bach's *St. Matthew Passion*, directed by Issay Dobrowen; on the 19th in Mozart's *Requiem*, directed by Guido Cantelli; on the 26th in Verdi's *Requiem* directed by Maestro Arturo Toscanini.

In July, she made her debut in Pompei, at the Teatro Grande, playing the role of Cleopatra in Handel's *Julius Caesar*, directed by Maestro Herbert Albert. Tito Ceccherini wrote in the *Corriere di Napoli* of 7 July 1950: "Tebaldi, one of the most beautiful, pure and bright voices ever in operatic singing, performed magnificently in the role of Cleopatra."

In September she left for Great Britain with the La Scala company. In Edinburgh's Husher Hall she sang Verdi's *Requiem*, directed by Victor de Sabata and Mozart's *Requiem*, directed by Cantelli. In London, at Covent Garden, she performed with Ramon Vinay, in *Otello*, and later in Verdi's *Requiem*, both times directed by Maestro De Sabata.

In September, Renata Tebaldi went on her first tour to the United States. She sang in *Aida* and in *Otello* and performed in a concert alongside Giuseppe di Stefano, in San Francisco. In Fresno, California, she made her debut with the role of the Countess of Almaviva in *Le Nozze di Figaro*. In Los Angeles, she sang in *Otello*, *Aida* and *Le Nozze di Figaro*.

Tebaldi opened the 1950–51 season at La Scala singing with Ramon Vinay in *Otello*, again directed by Victor de Sabata. On 3 February 1951, in the same theatre and under the same conductor, she performed as Violetta in *La Traviata*. After the final rehearsal one of Tebaldi's fans was sitting in the gallery. He recalls that as he was waiting for the artists to come out of the theatre in Via Filodrammatici, he saw Maestro De Sabata, who said: "You'll see. This time your Tebaldi has surpassed herself. When she sings she sounds like a violin."

The rehearsal, which had taken place behind closed doors, had been truly exceptional; but unfortunately on the evening of the premiere, the artist suffered from the effects of the stressful days and weeks before. During the preparation and the rehearsals of the opera, Tebaldi had, in fact, been engaged in two performances of the *Requiem Mass* organised to commemorate Verdi, and had also sung at the Teatro San Carlo, in Naples, in *Andrea Chénier*. On the night of the premiere, apart from being tired, she was bothered by the presence of several policemen backstage, who were watching her because she was wearing a very valuable diamond and ruby set the director had required for her role. In the first act, the singer missed the two "i gioir" and, in the final act, could not hold the top note in the aria "Addio del passato." The audience let out a murmur of surprise and disappointment. The singer still recalls that difficult moment vividly. She felt as if she had betrayed her audience; and that they did not dare reproach her but only out of affection.

Franco Abbiati wrote in the *Corriere della Sera* of 4 February: "Renata Tebaldi, with the sweetest, elegant, expressive and steady voice, got over the immense difficulties of Violetta's role, without wavering, expressing the full range of the qualities Dumas expected from the heroine of *Dame aux Camèlias*: devotion, passion, sorrow, resignation; all the different emotions a woman's heart might experience; calmness, serenity, dignity even in death. The first act—which covers the entire range of possible and impossible effects and accents for a soprano voice—exposed Tebaldi to some dangers, which she eluded more or less successfully. But the later acts (leaving aside the unexpected slip in the final one) proved how conscientiously and passionately this artist of ours studied and performed her character."

Renata Tebaldi's reaction was that of cancelling the other scheduled performances and took some time off to rest. She returned on stage in March 1951 at the Teatro San Carlo in Naples, performing once again in *La Traviata*. In his book *Voci Parallele*, Giacomo Lauri Volpi said: "In the same opera, the Teatro San Carlo di Napoli honoured her triumphantly." And he added an opinion on her voice: "Tebaldi's singing is caressing and soothing, rich in nuances, chiaroscuros. A style of singing which seems to dissolve her personality, as sugar dissolves in water making it sweeter, leaving no visible traces."

The day after the premiere, Alfredo Parente, in *Il Mattino* of 31 March 1951, started his review with the following heading: "Tebaldi's Time! *La Traviata* at the San Carlo with a new stage design. An unprecedented success and a sell-out." He wrote: "Renata Tebaldi responded with an example of the rarest, most exquisite versatility. With sublime

Renata Tebaldi together with Nicola Rossi Lemeni in a scene of Wagner's *Tannhäuser*, on stage at the Teatro San Carlo in Naples in 1948.

spontaneity, she departed from the great heights of her classical interpretations, empathising with the warm and pulsating humanity of the passionate character created by Verdi. She was able to grasp *Traviata*'s lively and sorrowful accents, her quivering abandon, pleasant expectations, despair, voluptuous exultation and gentle torment, with extraordinary vitality and spontaneous fresh enthusiasm. She showed her profound psychological intuition, capturing the sudden changes in mood and the slightest undertones of such a complex and voluble character. Renata Tebaldi, deeply moved by that triumph, a rare event indeed, went down on her knees to express her gratitude for such fervent acclamation. The audience continued to call for her, and shower her with bouquets thrown from the boxes."

The programme of the Teatro San Carlo of 23 April 1951 reads: "This aims at becoming a memento of an event. How else can one describe the event? This performance, which sees Renata Tebaldi in the leading female role, continues beyond the usual three evenings and, as in Rossini's crescendos, from the fourth night onwards, keeps drawing tireless theatre-goers who stand in line at the box office before dawn, fill the opera house up to the rafters, throw flowers to the singer on stage, and find the 'Sold-out' notice on the theatre doors, for nine days in a row. I couldn't tell who was more emotional at the end of the performance, the singer or the audience. And, if the schedule had permitted, this triumphal march would continue." After that sensational triumph, the theatre directors offered the artist a golden medal bearing on one side her portrait as Violetta and, on the other, the inscription "To Renata Tebaldi, who gave her enchanting voice and her pulsating heart to the immortal Violetta. A memento of a memorable success."

A. Procida wrote in *Il giornale di Napoli* on 31 March 1951: "What a miracle such a dramatic voice is, so pure and resonant and with such a remarkable volume. It's an intense voice that sweeps regal-

Tebaldi, playing the role of Elisabeth
in Wagner's *Tannhäuser,* on stage
at the Teatro San Carlo in Naples
in 1948, is wearing a large imitation
pearl, gilt metal and colourless
and green Bohemian crystal necklace
(on the opposite page) created
by Corbella in the 1940s.
The earrings, also by Corbella,
are part of the parure on page 189.

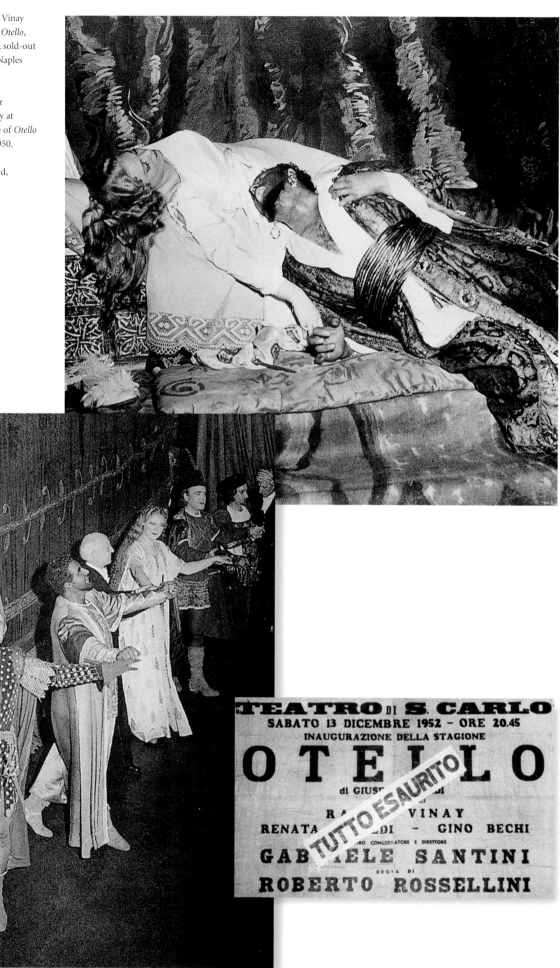

Renata Tebaldi and Ramon Vinay
in the final scene of Verdi's *Otello*,
director Roberto Rossellini, sold-out
at the Teatro San Carlo in Naples
on 13 December 1952.

Tebaldi with Maestro Victor
de Sabata and Ramon Vinay at
the end of the performance of *Otello*
at La Scala, in December 1950.

Opposite, in the background,
a smiling Renata Tebaldi.

TEATRO DI S. CARLO
SABATO 13 DICEMBRE 1952 - ORE 20.45
INAUGURAZIONE DELLA STAGIONE
OTELLO
di GIUSE   DI
RA   VINAY
RENATA   DI - GINO BECHI
     CONCERTATORE E DIRETTORE
GAB ELE SANTINI
REGIA DI
ROBERTO ROSSELLINI

TUTTO ESAURITO

ly over a vast range, easily bent to the virtuosity of a soprano, with unusual elegance and delightful smoothness. We have to go back to Muzio to find a similar phenomenon; and, yet, Tebaldi is a greater singer; an actress that gives life to her character, suffers along with it and idealises it, as she has shown superbly in the unforgettable, sublime duet with Georgio Germont, in the second act."

At the beginning of June, Tebaldi sang again at La Scala, alongside Mariano Stabile, in *Falstaff*, conducted by Victor de Sabata. At the end of June and in July, she went to Paris to sing, with the theatrical company of the Teatro San Carlo, for the Giuseppe Verdi commemoration. On the 30th, she sang in *Giovanna d'Arco* at the Opéra, and on 5 July she was at the Madeleine in the *Requiem Mass*.

From August to October, Tebaldi was on tour in Brazil, singing in *La Traviata, La Bohème, Aida,* and *Andrea Chénier*, as well as in *Tosca* and in Verdi's *Requiem*. She also performed at a concert at the Teatro Municipal of Rio de Janeiro.

By the end of December, she was again at the Teatro San Carlo in Naples, where she made her debut as Amazily in Spontini's *Fernando Cortez*. The same opera house saw her as Pamira, on 2 January 1952, in Gioacchino Rossini's *L'Assedio di Corinto*.

Tebaldi returned to La Scala in April, with *Mefistofele* and, in May, with *Falstaff*, both conducted by Victor de Sabata. The soprano gave her first performance in the role of Matilde, in Rossini's *Guglielmo Tell* and, on 26 December, she closed the season at the Teatro San Carlo, giving her first performance in Francesco Cilea's *Adriana Lecouvreur*. The following day, *Il Mattino* reported: "Adriana has turned fifty; yet, real masterpieces such as *Adriana* shall never age. For this anniversary, as the author has futilely desired so many times before, Adriana was sung by Renata Tebaldi. Now, knowing the fine artist Tebaldi is, it is not difficult to guess how she brought Cilea's character of Adriana to life. There was thunderous frequent applause during the most famous passages of the opera."

Tebaldi remained very fond of the character of Adriana, which was to become one of her hallmarks. Throughout her career she sang the part in the most important theatres, from La Scala to Barcelona's Gran Teatro del Liceo, from the Lyric Opera of Chicago to the Auditorium de la Habana.

Tebaldi, playing the role of Elisabeth
in Wagner's *Tannhäuser*, on stage
at the Teatro San Carlo in Naples
in 1948, with the same stage jewels
worn in *Otello*. The artist loved
interpreting the role of Desdemona
more than any other, and has always
been very fond of the stage jewellery
she wore in occasion of her debut.

The jewels created by Corbella in the
1940s, in gilt metal, multi-coloured
Bohemian crystals and imitation
pearls, worn by Renata Tebaldi
in *Otello* and in *Tannhäuser*.

At Rome's Teatro dell'Opera, Tebaldi had great success on many occasions. Nino Piccinelli, writing in *Momento sera* on 13 April 1962, noted: "The leading role, so elaborate in its vocal and scenic requirements, has found in Renata Tebaldi a performer with natural expressiveness. Toscanini used to say that she has 'the voice of an angel' and last night, in the role of Adriana, the artist was simply sensational. Across the entire melodic spectrum of the main character's lyric expressions, Tebaldi's voice shone with the brightness of thousands of lights. Her acting was also superb, a true embodiment of her character. An emotional audience—elegant and knowledgeable—received the 'national Renata' so enthusiastically, a rare occurrence in our great Opera House."

To grant Tebaldi's request, Rudolph Bing, general manager of the Metropolitan Opera of New York, put *Adriana* back on the programme in 1963, fifty years after its first performance, and again, for the opening of the 1968 opera season. On 18 September 1968 the *Progresso Italo-Americano* reported: "The return of *Adriana Lecouvreur* for the opening night of the Metropolitan Opera is the mission of a great artist, Renata Tebaldi, who has been loyal to the opera as to the greatest achievement in her career … *Adriana* requires great performers, especially in the leading role. The character is permeated with the pangs of love, or rather of passion, and the premonition of death. Only a great dramatic actress and a formidable singer is capable of grasping the rhythm in the passages from tender bliss to furious resentment, from sweet abandon to the fatal blow."

Tebaldi also fondly recalls the evening of 16 September 1968 because of another important event, the great reconciliation with her long-time rival, Maria Callas. A rivalry which started back in 1950 and gave the international press much to write about, dividing opera lovers into two separate groups: the Tebaldi fans and the Callas fans, whose arguments typified one of the most exciting moments in the history of modern opera. Renata Tebaldi recalls: "After the performance, Rudolph Bing came to congratulate me and told me, 'There's a dear friend who would like to greet you.' And I asked, 'Is it Zinca Milanov?' 'No,' he replied, 'It's Maria.' I said nothing for a minute and then told him I would be glad to meet her. I saw Maria near the door of Franco Corelli's dressing room. You could tell she was emotional. I went up to her and we hugged each other; she told me she hoped I

With Herbert von Karajan
in Vienna, in 1958, at the end
of a *Tosca* conducted by the Maestro.

Renata Tebaldi next to Rudolph Bing
at the Metropolitan Opera in New
York, in the 1960s.

Renata Tebaldi in the role
of Adriana Lecouvreur,
photographed by Saez in 1962,
at the Teatro Coliseo Alba in Bilbao.
She is wearing stage jewels created
in imitation turquoise *pâte de verre*
and imitation diamond colourless
crystals.The set shown on the right
is made up of necklace, earrings
and ring.

Renata Tebaldi

Renata Tebaldi with Di Costanzo, general manager of the Teatro San Carlo in Naples during the historic *La Traviata* performance, in 1951. Behind them are the stage curtains decorated with fresh camellias as requested by Di Costanzo in honour of Tebaldi, whom he had a high regard for. On that occasion, the theatre directors offered the artist a golden medal, bearing her portrait as Violetta on one side and on the other the inscription: "To Renata Tebaldi, who gave her enchanting voice and her pulsating heart to the immortal Violetta. A memento of a memorable success."

In the second scene of act 2, the soprano wore the tiara of the parure (on the opposite page) created by Corbella in the 1940s in silver-plated metal and colourless Bohemian crystals.

Renata Tebaldi

Necklace created by Ennio Marino
Marangoni for the role of Floria
Tosca in a *Tosca* performance
conducted by Maestro De Sabata
which went on stage in Milan
on 12 April 1953, during a gala
evening at La Scala.

Renata Tebaldi as Floria Tosca
at La Scala in Milan.

In the background, Tebaldi is
shown with Maestro De Sabata
and Giuseppe di Stefano.

Renata Tebaldi

191

would be as happy and as successful as I had been that evening. I felt rather sorry for Maria, whose love life had been unhappy, like mine, as a few months earlier Aristoteles Onassis had left her. The next day, I phoned her at Hotel Pierre, but she had already left. So, I decided to write her a letter, she answered inviting me to go and see her when I was in Paris."

The two artists never met again and Maria Callas died exactly nine years after that meeting—on 16 September 1977.

In January 1953 Tebaldi made her debut in Licinio Refice's *Cecilia*, in Naples, at the Teatro San Carlo, directed by the composer himself. She had numerous engagements that year: among the most important ones, a magnificent *Tosca* at La Scala directed by Victor de Sabata and, as part of the Maggio Musicale Fiorentino, her debut as Leonora in Verdi's *La Forza del Destino*, alongside Mario del Monaco, directed by Dimitri Mitropoulus.

On 7 December she performed *Wally* at La Scala for the opening of the 1953–54 season. Subsequently, Tebaldi sang again at La Scala, with Mario del Monaco, in *Otello*, *Tosca,* and—in May—she premiered in the role of Tatiana in Tchaikowsky's *Eugene Onegin*, conducted by Maestro Artur Rodzinski.

In January 1955 she left for the United States. She would make her debut at the Metropolitan Opera, in New York, performing in *Otello*, alongside Mario del Monaco and Leonard Warren, under the direction of Fritz Stiedry. Critics wrote: "America's New Opera Sensation." Henry Lang wrote in the *New York Herald Tribune* on 1st February 1955: "Renata Tebaldi, the famous Italian soprano, made her debut … A voice able to soar above the volume of the orchestra, and flutter pure and clear. And yet, her *pianissimo* was heard perfectly across the large hall, because it does not murmur but is a full musical sound, beautifully rendered."

On the same day, Louis Biancolli wrote in the *New York World Telegram*: "Renata Tebaldi, the greatly acclaimed queen of Italian sopranos made a sensational debut last night, at the Metropolitan Opera playing Desdemona in Verdi's *Otello* … The performance proves Miss Tebaldi's talent. Her voice is beautiful, full and steady. She can play with an infinite range of nuances. Her voice has the necessary colour to adapt to a succession of emotions and

Renata Tebaldi is Adriana Lecouvreur
at the Teatro Liceo de Barcelona, in
1958.

In 1954 at La Scala, singing the role
of Tatiana in Tchaikowsky's *Eugene
Onegin*, next to baritone Ettore
Bastianini and director Tatjana
Pavlova.

Renata Tebaldi photographed
in New York, in 1956, together with
Elsa Maxwell.

Renata Tebaldi in New York in 1967, with costume designer Beni Montresor who created the costume for the role of Manon Lescaut, worn by the artist in occasion of her debut at the Metropolitan Opera.
Next to them, the costumer Ray Diffen, specialized in stage costumes. To create this magnificent outfit (next page), which required many months of work, she used eighteen meters of silk brocade imported directly from Formosa.

imagination. Sounds have always given warmth and brilliance to the crescendo fabric of the great Verdian tapestry of destiny. At all times she controlled her voice superbly from the silent, celestial *pianissimos* of the love music and devotional music, to the stunning high notes expressing shame and terror. Renata Tebaldi is a top-class musician and an artist of rare perfection. She was an imploring, sweet and passionate Desdemona and, when her dignity was offended, she was stirring, majestic. She has been criticised as a singer, as an artist, personally. It surely seems that, last night, Rudolph Bing selected another winner."

After the success with *Otello*, she sang again in

February in *La Bohème, Andrea Chénier* and, in March in *Tosca*. In April she went back to Italy to perform in Verdi's *La Forza del Destino* at La Scala, where she would not return for the next four years. Tebaldi had her greatest success on the many occasions she performed at the Metropolitan Opera, in 1957, with a magnificent *La Bohème*.

In the *New York Journal-American*, Elsa Maxwell wrote on 16 February 1957: "Last week an angel flew down from the sky to the stage of the Metropolitan with a golden harp in her throat, not in her hand. That angel was, of course, the great Tebaldi who sang—as only she can sing—the pathetic role of Mimì, in *La Bohème*." The critic added that the artist

Renata Tebaldi

Tebaldi fitting stage costumes for
costumer Rolf Gérard for *La Traviata*
on stage at the Metropolitan Opera
in New York in 1957.

Tebaldi wearing the costume
for scene 2, act 2. In the background,
the sketch for the costume.

Renata Tebaldi

Necklace created by Miriam Haskell in the 1950s with Baroque imitation pearls, gilt metal and crystals, which Tebaldi wore in act 1 of *La Traviata* performed in 1957 at the Metropolitan Opera in New York. Act 1 required a different pearl necklace, which the artist wore during the first performance. Then, Tebaldi saw the necklace created by Haskell in a shop and decided to purchase it and wear it in all the subsequent performances.

Renata Tebaldi

Renata Tebaldi in the role of Tosca
on the cover of *Time* magazine,
in November 1958. She was wearing
the tiara specially made for her
by Ennio Marino Marangoni.

The tiara created by Marangoni
in gilt metal, colourless Swarovski
crystals and imitation ruby red
crystals.

A dramatic photograph of Renata
Tebaldi in the final act of *La Traviata*,
on stage at the Metropolitan Opera
in New York in 1957.

In the background, a close-up
of a radiant young Tebaldi.

The jewels created in 1961 by Ennio Marino Marangoni to a design by Nicola Benois for the character of Fedora Ramazov in *Fedora,* performed at the Teatro San Carlo in Naples in December 1961. The set Renata Tebaldi wore when she played the role of the Princess included a tiara, a brooch with pendant in the shape of a large Orthodox cross, a pair of earrings and a ring. The set was made of gilt metal and entirely decorated with colourless, red and aquamarine Swarovski crystals. When Benois, who was born in St. Petersburg, created the magnificent brooch, he was, perhaps, inspired by a photograph of Queen Maria of Romania, niece of Tzar Alexander II of Russia, who had a jewel very similar to this one.

Renata Tebaldi

was left standing alone on the stage for a much deserved ovation—something that had occurred there only twice before: "And the thunderous applause brought the roof down, and Tebaldi was left alone on the stage, overwhelmed by the warmth of the great acclamation." *Newsweek* of 18 February 1957 reported: "Renata Tebaldi was received with the most extraordinary and spontaneous ovation ever given to any other singer this season. The Italian soprano received such rapturous applause that even the shouts of her fans were muffled."

On 21 February she sang the role of Violetta in *La Traviata*, an opera that had not been on that stage since 1935. There were great expectations for that event, which will go down in the history of the Metropolitan Opera. The enthusiastic audience started tearing down the floral decorations in the hall and tossed flowers onto the stage. Louis Biancolli wrote in the *New York World Telegram* of 22 February 1957: "Renata Tebaldi's premiered a *Traviata* at the Metropolitan, which turned yesterday's performance into a second opening of the season … She was Violetta—a delight to the eyes, the ears and the soul."

Robert Coleman wrote in the *Daily Mirror*: "In the middle register she had a velvety voice. The high notes were accurate, vibrant and brilliant. The electric Tebaldi sparkles through the spotlights. There have been few singers this decade who have had such scores of faithful followers. Each one of her performances at the Metropolitan becomes as important as the opening season galas due to her magnetism and high-class artistry." Outside the theatre there were mounted police to keep the crowd of admirers waiting to see the artist under control.

On 27 October 1958 at the opening of the 75th season at the Metropolitan Opera, with *Tosca* Renata Tebaldi won the same enthusiastic acclaim from the public. The opera house was so full, that the beginning of the performance had to be delayed. That night the Metropolitan box-office had record takings. Her success was extraordinary, and *Time* magazine dedicated a cover to her as Tosca. In the *Daily Mirror* Robert Coleman wrote, on 28 October 1958: "Renata Tebaldi embodied the main character magnificently. Her miming was evocative; her singing exceptionally beautiful, inspired by an extraordinary opening evening. Tebaldi started singing 'Vissi d'arte,' a test bench for Tosca, with an almost contemplative composure, developing the aria to reach a powerful peak. She re-

A magnificent Renata Tebaldi receiving the applause of her audience at the Metropolitan Opera, in New York, after singing the aria "Io son l'umile ancella" from Cilea's Adriana Lecouvreur, performed in September 1968.

ceived an outburst of 'brava!'" In *The New York Times* Howard Taubman wrote on the same day: "Her voice is still one of the most exceptional instruments of our time."

Two more debuts are linked to the history of opera theatre of New York, namely: on 16 September 1966 the new Metropolitan Lincoln Centre was inaugurated with Samuel Barber's *Antony and Cleopatra*; and on 22 September, by many considered to be the real opening, Ponchielli's *Gioconda* went on stage, and Tebaldi premiered in the leading role, with Franco Corelli. The *World Critical Tribune* reported on 23 September 1966: "A triumph for Tebaldi … It was an absolutely unbelievable performance of Renata Tebaldi in the title role. She has proved to have developed on stage a new self-possession, when, last night, she used her voice to attempt things she had never tried before. On the same day *The New York Post* stated: "Tebaldi, as beautiful as ever, performed her first Gioconda. In spite of the sharpness of her voice she portrayed her character perfectly. Dark colours in the aria of the suicide scene emphasised the macabre atmosphere. Her phrasing was always markedly sensitive."

Renata Tebaldi made another debut with Puccini's *La Fanciulla del West* in 1970. Harold Schönberg wrote: "Today, New York has found a new 'Fanciulla del West' to fall in love with." By this time the Metropolitan had been a sell-out for fifteen years every time she performed; Tebaldi, was in fact, nicknamed "Miss Sold-out."

In 1973, Renata Tebaldi sang for the last time at the Metropolitan Opera, in *Otello*, and then began a tour of concerts in the United States and in Russia. On 23 May 1976 she performed in a concert at La Scala, which was a tribute to the people of Friuli devastated by an earthquake. The public responded warmly. The *Corriere di Milano* on 24 May 1976 reported: "Tebaldi has once again been able to attract crowds of fans, all those who have always cherished her pure and perfect voice in their hearts. Renata repaid them by singing for two hours, causing, at times, uncontrollable enthusiasm." Shortly after that concert, Renata Tebaldi called up the pianist who used to go every day to her house for scale practising and she simply said: "Please don't come any more. I have decided to stop singing."

It was a mere coincidence that the date of her last concert and her last public performance coincided with the day of her first performance in Rovigo thirty-two years earlier.

Concise Bibliography

C. M. Casanova, *Renata Tebaldi. La voce d'angelo*, Venice 1981
F. Degrada (edited by), *Verdi e la Scala*, Milan 2001
M. Galli de Furlani (for the Italian edition), *Il mondo della musica*, Milan 1961
C. Gatti, *Il Teatro alla Scala nella storia e nell'arte (1758-1958)*, Milan 1963
L. Pennati, G. Asnicar (edited by), *Gocciole d'astri. I monili del melodramma*, Milan 1991
E. Respighi, *Ottorino Respighi*, Milan 1954

Photographic Credits

Most of the photographs published in this volume are from the Author's collection. The others are through the kind permission of:

Her Royal Highness Maria Gabriella di Savoia
Margherita Carosio
Rosanna Carteri
Antonietta Stella
Renata Tebaldi

Archivio Corbella, Milan
Archivio Maggio Musicale Fiorentino, Florence
Archivio Teatro alla Scala, Milan
Roberto Devalle, Turin
Fondazione Umberto II
e Maria José di Savoia, Geneva
Maestro Pier Luigi Pizzi, Rome
Olympia Publifoto, Milan
Dario Tettamanzi, Milan

Acknowledgements

*I would like to thank
Valeria Alemà Regazzoni,
Bruno Bani, Marzia Berchielli,
Michela Beretta, Sara Boioli,
Angelo Cereda, Angelo Corbella,
Mario De Carlo, Melissa Gabardi,
Caterina Giavotto, Maria Maio,
Muzzino, Massimo Navoni,
Simona Oreglia, Sara Salvi,
Dario Tagliabue, Dario Tettamanzi,
Barbara Travaglini, Tina Viganò,
Lucia Vigo
who have kindly collaborated
in the production of this book*

*My most grateful thanks
and my affection to
Margherita Carosio, Rosanna Carteri,
Antonietta Stella, Renata Tebaldi,
without whose valuable help this work
would never have been possible (S.P.)*

Cover
A casacade of multi-coloured Swarovski and Bohemian crystals
(photograph by Dario Tettamanzi)

Back cover
Margherita Carosio, Rosanna Carteri, Antonietta Stella,
Renata Tebaldi

On pages 4–5
Original drawing by Maestro Pier Luigi Pizzi
for the costumes for Handel's *Orlando*
for the 1959 Maggio Musicale Fiorentino

On page 8
Early 20th century bracelet by Corbella with *pâte de verre*
and others in imitation turquoise; next to it, moulds
and other instruments for making stage jewels,
also belonging to the Corbella workshop

Art Director
Dario Tagliabue

Page Layout
Sara Salvi

Editorial Coordination
Caterina Giavotto

Editing
Simona Oreglia

Technical Coordination
Mario Farè

Quality Control
Giancarlo Berti

Translations
David Giddings (forewords)
Maria Rosaria Buri
with Catherine Biggerstaff

www.electaweb.it

This volume was printed for Mondadori Electa S.p.A.
by Martellago Mondadori Printing S.p.A.
Via Castellana 98, Martellago (Venice) in the year 2004